Books by Hershel Shanks

Jerusalem's Temple Mount: From Solomon to the Golden Dome (forthcoming)

Jerusalem: An Archaeological Biography

The Mystery and Meaning of the Dead Sea Scrolls

The City of David: A Guide to Biblical Jerusalem

Judaism in Stone: The Archaeology of Ancient Synagogues

The Dead Sea Scrolls After Forty Years (with James C. VanderKam, P. Kyle McCarter, Jr., and James A. Sanders)

The Rise of Ancient Israel (with William G. Dever, Baruch Halpern and P. Kyle McCarter, Jr.)

Books Edited by Hershel Shanks

Ancient Israel: A Short History from Abraham to the Roman Destruction of the Temple

The Art and Craft of Judging: The Opinions of Judge Learned Hand

Christianity and Rabbinic Judaism: A Parallel History of Their Origins and Early Development

Understanding the Dead Sea Scrolls

Archaeology and the Bible: The Best of BAR, 2 vols. (with Dan P. Cole)

Feminist Approaches to the Bible (with Phyllis Trible, Tikva Frymer-Kensky, Pamela J. Milne and Jane Schaberg)

Recent Archaeology in the Land of Israel (with Benjamin Mazar)

The Search for Jesus (with Stephen J. Patterson, Marcus J. Borg and John Dominic Crossan)

The City of David: Revisiting Early Excavations (with Ronny Reich)

The
Copper
Scroll
and the
Search for
the Temple
Treasure

HERSHEL SHANKS

BIBLICAL ARCHAEOLOGY SOCIETY

Library of Congress Cataloging-in-Publication Data

Shanks, Hershel.

The Copper scroll and the search for the Temple treasure / Hershel Shanks.

p. cm.

Includes bibliographical references.

ISBN 978-0-9796357-1-7

1. Copper scroll. 2. Treasure troves—Palestine. I. Title.

BM488.C6S53 2007

296.1'55—dc22

2007016497

© 2007 Biblical Archaeology Society
4710 41st Street, NW
Washington, DC 20016

Table of Contents

List of Illustrations

Acknowledgments

This book, like all Biblical Archaeology Society productions, is essentially a staff effort. And it is a little unfair that only one name appears as the author.

Moreover, much of the staff effort is joint effort, not just one person doing one thing and another doing something else. It is all working together in the best sense. The following description of the various contributions does not capture the warm nature of this overall cooperative effort.

The direction of the project was, as usual, in the capable hands of our publisher Susan Laden.

All editorial questions that arose in the course of writing and producing this book were turned over to *Biblical Archaeology Review* assistant editor Dorothy D. Resig. She was in charge of obtaining the pictures and picture permissions and wrote the captions to the illustrations. The maps in this book also come from her talented hand.

Administrative editor Bonnie Mullin researched several difficult questions until she got to the bottom of disputed points. The endnotes entirely belong to her.

Editorial associate Meghan Dombrink-Green ably assisted with much of the research.

My long-time colleague, web editor Steven Feldman, significantly improved the language of some of the text.

After more than 30 years, we continue to make use of our design director Rob Sugar, who supervised the amply creative efforts of art director David Fox and designer Melissa Kelly. They made the basic decisions regarding the design of the book as well as the dust jacket.

Production manager Heather Metzger handled the overall production and manufacture of the book so seamlessly and efficiently that we hardly noticed that it was being done.

What we lack, however, is the expertise and scholarship that only the academy can provide. Fortunately we were able to call on two long-time friends, Professor George J. Brooke of The University of Manchester in Manchester, England, and Professor P. Kyle McCarter of The Johns Hopkins University in Baltimore, Maryland, who graciously reviewed the manuscript to rid it of its most glaring errors. The remaining glitches derive from my sometimes unwillingness to follow their sage advice.

I am especially grateful to Professor McCarter and to Professor James H. Charlesworth of Princeton Theological Seminary and director of the Princeton Theological Seminary Dead Sea Scrolls Project for permission to reprint in an appendix (and to quote throughout) Professor McCarter's translation of the Copper Scroll prepared for a future volume of the project.

Hershel Shanks
Washington, D.C.
May 2007

Foreword

The title is not the only element of this book that hints of Indiana Jones. Inviting the reader on an inductive study to correct long-held deductions, Shanks tells a tale with all of the intrigue, animosity and revenge of a murder mystery. Approaching the subject with the acumen of a lawyer, rather than as a seasoned Scroll scholar embroiled in the usual "squabbles," Shanks is a fresh, unencumbered voice on the scene.

He examines and cross-examines the many attempts to chip away at different facets of the Copper Scroll: first the dramatic race between the resourceful Bedouin and the modern Europeans to excavate the scrolls in desert caves, and then among often-ruthless scholars aspiring to lay claim to some aspect of the scrolls' discovery, and finally the gold-diggers' current race for the legendary Temple treasure. The Copper Scroll's extensive inventory of buried treasure may be sober, but Shanks's investigation is gripping and makes the reader privy to decoded secrets.

A Scroll scholar and even a mildly interested reader will find this dramatic story to be a page-turner. (Was I holding my breath anticipating the winners in each of these areas?) I knew the outcomes, but I imagined both the defeats and victories anew in Shanks's vivid retelling that adds just enough information to avoid both over-simplification and pedantic complexity. Interest will mount and you'll want to read more about this "cold case," a "file" that Shanks considers "perhaps the most intriguing and puzzling found among the 900 documents known collectively as the Dead Sea Scrolls."

As a student of William Foxwell Albright at the time the scrolls were discovered, I was among the first to learn of this unprecedented revelation in biblical studies. The field changed overnight. I was assigned to translate the Leviticus Scroll, which I found intriguing because it was one of two scrolls written in paleo-Hebrew, a more ancient form of Hebrew, and probably considered more "sacred."

Then in 1960, John Allegro and I co-authored *The Treasure of the Copper Scroll*, which contained the first facsimile and translation of the text intended for the general public. After more than 40 years, the enigmas remain and have even multiplied. (Does the Scroll mention a possible connection to Jesus Christ? Is the treasure real or imagined? Why is it so clumsily engraved?) More recently, I published the primer *What Are the Dead Sea Scrolls and Why Do They Matter?* (Eerdmans, 2007), which mentions the Copper Scroll. But this scroll deserves careful scrutiny in another full-length treatment.

The difficulty of unrolling, cutting, bending and prying open the Copper Scroll is as intricate a process as Shanks's examination of the facts surrounding the enigmatic treasure. Shanks thoroughly addresses all of the major concerns surrounding the Copper Scroll, and each of his comprehensive propositions necessarily excavates compelling new questions.

From its creation 2,000 years ago, to the first time a scholar saw the clumsy lettering on the copper sheet in 1948, later to be sawed into 23 strips, surfacing in news leaks and "pirated" publications, the Copper Scroll remains veiled in intrigue. Shanks dramatizes the race to find out if the scroll really means what it says, and he equips us to reasonably consider these very issues.

You rest your case, counselor.

David Noel Freedman
University of California, San Diego
May 2007

Introduction

The majority of scholars believes that the Copper Scroll describes the treasure of the Jerusalem Temple. Shortly before 70 C.E., when the Roman legions burned the city and its holy sanctuary, this treasure was buried at more than 60 sites designated in the Copper Scroll.

This book is the story of that scroll.

Scholars rarely vote on such things. But in this case, they did. At a conference of experts held in Manchester, England, where the Copper Scroll was opened more than 50 years ago, a poll of the scholars in attendance found that "the majority opinion was that in some way this wealth [of buried treasure] should be connected with the Jerusalem Temple."[1]

Among the approximately 900 Dead Sea Scrolls, the Copper Scroll is the only one whose text is hammered on copper. All the other scrolls are written in ink on animal skins or papyrus.

Among the Dead Sea Scrolls, the Copper Scroll is the only autograph; that is, an original composition, not a copy of some other text. Only four or five Dead Sea Scrolls are complete. The Copper Scroll is one of them. The treasure of the Copper Scroll has never been found. But the search goes on.

This book is also the story of that search.

[1]George J. Brooke in George J. Brooke and Philip R. Davies, eds., *Copper Scroll Studies*, *Journal for the Study of the Pseudepigrapha*, Supplement Series 40 (Sheffield, England: Sheffield Academic Press, 2002), p. 8.

CHAPTER 1

The Scholars Win One

For the Ta'amireh Bedouin who accidentally discovered the first seven Dead Sea Scrolls in a cave near
Qumran in the Judean Desert, the race was on. They
wanted more. Curiously, the scholars did not react
this way. For them, the Bedouin's discovery had been a one-
time bit of luck. Finding other caves with other scrolls was
highly unlikely, they reasoned, hardly worth the effort. Instead,
they began excavating the nearby site of Qumran in the hope of
better understanding the contents of the scrolls and their possible relationship to the site.

The initial seven intact scrolls first came to scholarly attention in 1947. By February 1949 an archaeological expedition
under the direction of Father Roland de Vaux of the École Biblique et Archéologique Française in Jerusalem and G. Lankester Harding, the British head of the Jordanian Department
of Antiquities, was in the field at Qumran, enlisting some of the
Bedouin looters as workers.

Not realizing that their chance find in what later became known as Qumran Cave 1 was likely to be a single, unique occasion, the Bedouin continued to search the nearby caves for more scrolls when they were not in the field excavating with de Vaux. In 1951 their search again proved successful. They found Cave 2 not far from Cave 1, both about a mile north of the ruins of Qumran. Although Cave 2 held only a few fragments, these fragments (along with texts found by the Bedouin in a cave several miles south of Qumran from a later period) were enough to convince the scholars that they had been wrong and that it might be worthwhile to search other caves for more scrolls.

So the competition began, the Bedouin against the scholars. The scholars seemed to have the advantage. They were accustomed to reasoning things out. They had known since January 1949 the location of Cave 1: Harding had sent a military unit of the famed Arab League to scour the general area where the documents had supposedly been discovered. After a two- or three-day search, an Arab captain noticed freshly turned dirt in front of a small cave opening. When the cave was explored, 70 small fragments of scrolls were found, including fragments of two of the original seven intact scrolls, thus confirming that this was the site of the original discovery. Moreover, the scholars also knew the location of nearby Cave 2: When fragments from this cave came onto the market, the Bedouin had agreed to take the scholars to the site.

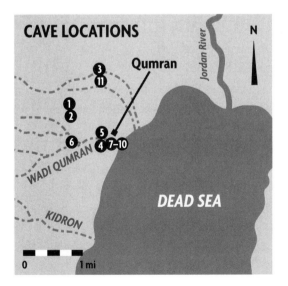

All told, 11 caves containing scroll fragments were discovered in the vicinity of Qumran. They were named Caves 1–11 based on the order in which they were found.

While looking for his lost sheep in a cave, a Bedouin shepherd named Muhammad edh-Dhib, "the Wolf," (pictured on the right with his cousin) discovered seven intact scrolls that later became known as the Dead Sea Scrolls.

Finally, convinced that it was worthwhile searching other caves, in March 1952 the scholars organized the Qumran Cave Expedition led by de Vaux. The scholars cleverly observed that both Cave 1 and Cave 2 were in the limestone cliffs high above Qumran. So their expedition made forays into more than 250 caves—all in the limestone cliffs.

The less-sophisticated Bedouin did not confine their search

The ruins of Qumran sit on the marl terrace overlooking the Wadi Qumran.

Father Roland de Vaux, a Dominican priest from the École Biblique et Archéologique Française in Jerusalem, was co-director of the Qumran excavations and the first editor-in-chief of the scroll-publication team.

to the limestone cliffs. They also looked in caves in the soft marl terrace between the limestone cliffs and the flatland on the shore of the Dead Sea.

As might be expected, the Bedouin almost always won the competition to find more scrolls. The famous Cave 4, which contained the mother lode, was discovered by the Bedouin in the marl terrace almost within the ruins of Qumran, literally under the noses of the archaeologists digging nearby. Cave 4 held nearly 600 different scrolls, although all in tatters. By the time the archaeologists discovered the Bedouin excavating Cave 4, over 80 percent of the fragments had been removed. The archaeologists were left essentially with a mopping-up operation.

In an interview in 1993, I asked Harvard's Frank Cross, who was a member of the initial scroll-publication team, "Why the hell didn't you look in the marl terrace?" Cross replied:

> Don't look at me. I was not with the teams of explorers. I came to Jerusalem after Cave 4 was discovered. I guess

Thousands of scroll fragments were ultimately discovered in the caves around Khirbet Qumran. While the caves in the limestone cliffs were naturally formed, others—such as Caves 4 and 5, seen here—were man-made, dug into the marl terrace.

the leaders of the scholarly expedition that searched for caves thought that, given limited time and money, their best chance of finding more scrolls was in the kind of terrain and type of cave where previous finds had been made. Had I been on the team of exploration, I probably would have reasoned, alas, as they did. The Bedouin were brighter and more flexible.[1]

The archaeologists did have one victory, however. It was they who discovered Cave 3 in the limestone cliffs northeast of Caves 1 and 2.

The caves in the limestone cliffs are much different from those in the marl. The latter appear to be man-made. They were often living quarters in antiquity. The caves in the limestone cliffs, on the other hand, are the work of nature. They are dank and smelly. And their shape is random—high then low (watch your head), not level or straight or round, wide then narrow (you may have to squeeze through on the ground), not easy to identify, sometimes with the only opening high on the cliff, sometimes entirely concealed by rock fall. Finally, they can be

Cave 4 was discovered by the Bedouin and contained the mother lode, but all in fragments. After Bedouin looted the cave, archaeologists did a clean-up excavation. Approximately 15,000 fragments comprising more than 500 documents were recovered from this cave alone.

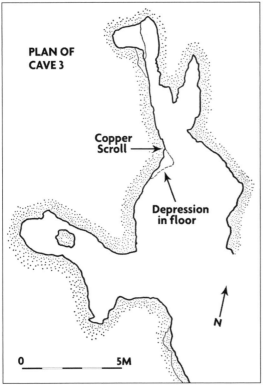

PLAN OF CAVE 3

Copper Scroll →

↗ Depression in floor

↑ N

0 _____ 5M

In 1952 scholars finally caught a break with the discovery of Cave 3. In addition to several scroll fragments, the cave produced a most unusual find: the Copper Scroll.

huge, with several halls in varying directions.

Such is the case with Cave 3, which was explored from March 14 to March 25, 1952, by one of de Vaux's groups led by a French expert in the Neolithic period named Henri de Contenson. Even the original entrance to the cave is not certain today.[2] Parts of the cave collapsed centuries after ancient artifacts and manuscripts had been deposited in it. More recent collapse—perhaps a few centuries ago—confused things still further. The caves are all located in the Great Rift Valley—where two tectonic plates come together—which runs from Africa up the Jordan Valley and continues northward into Syria, so earthquakes are common here.

Despite the rock collapse (and the work of a nest of rodents that devoured much of the manuscripts), the archaeologists recovered several important scroll fragments from Cave 3: some from the Book of the prophet Ezekiel, others from the Book of Psalms, and still other fragments from works such as Jubilees, one of which refers to "an angel of peace." All together, the scholars identified 14 different documents from the cave.

Once they supposedly emptied Cave 3, the scholars decided that it might be worthwhile to have one more look. At that

When the archaeologists were nearly done excavating Cave 3, a small ledge was discovered behind some fallen rock. Nestled on that ledge were two rolls of thin copper sheet that became known as the Copper Scroll.

point, some members of the exploration group noticed ancient pottery sherds in a depression of a slope in the cave. Behind the sherds was a huge rock that had collapsed from the roof of the cave and now barred the entrance to what appeared to be a small cave behind it. The explorers chipped away at the rock until they had cleared a narrow entrance to this side cave at the northern end of the main cave. On March 20, 1952, squeezing inside the small cave, they discovered a natural shelf in the back on which had been deposited two copper rolls, each about a foot long. Some time after the rolls had been placed there, the roof collapsed, effectively secreting them for 2,000 years.

It is those rolls that are the subject of this book. Constituting the Copper Scroll, they are perhaps the most intriguing and puzzling of all the more than 900 documents known collectively as the Dead Sea Scrolls.

CHAPTER 2

From Rolls to Scrolls

I t was not immediately apparent that these copper tubes were a scroll. Nothing like them had ever been discovered before. Indeed, nothing like them has been discovered since. They are, after all, made of metal, 99 percent pure copper, not something that is easily rolled and unrolled like a leather or papyrus scroll.

Because they cannot be rolled and unrolled, Father Joseph Fitzmyer, a leading Dead Sea Scroll scholar, says these rolls are "not really a scroll at all."[1] It might be more accurate to call them a plaque (or, at this point in our story, two plaques).

From the ends of the two tubes, however, it was clear that thin sheets of copper had been rolled up. Careful examination and computation determined that the shorter of the rolls was about 2.5 feet long, and the longer one twice that. Together they measured nearly 8 feet long.

The scholars noticed some letters extruded on the outside of the rolls. It was clear that there was writing inside—and it was Hebrew. The letters had been beaten into the metal with a sharp instrument—naturally they appeared in reverse on the outside.

The copper was completely oxidized and extremely brittle. At the slightest touch, the metal could crumble into dust. And no one seemed to know how to open the rolls without at the same time destroying them.

In the spring of 1953, about a year after the two rolls had been recovered from Cave 3, a German professor named Karl George Kuhn of Göttingen University visited the Palestine Archaeological Museum (now the Rockefeller Museum) in Jerusalem, where the rolls were on exhibit. Although he was a competent and highly respected scholar, he was allowed to examine the rolls only in the showcase. Despite this restriction, Kuhn decided to study the extruded letters to see what he might discover. With the help of mirrors and photographs, Kuhn deciphered 220 letters comprising more than 50 words. Later examination determined that 90 percent of Kuhn's identifications were correct. Among the 50 words he identified were five appearances of the word "dig" at so many "cubits" from something, as well as the word "gold." From this point on, it was generally assumed that the text related to buried treasure, raising to a new level the fascination and mystery of what may now be called the Copper Scroll.

But "none of this is certain, of course," Kuhn wrote. "These are more or less probable deductions stemming from a limited textual basis. But if we want to advance in new research, we must have the courage to draw surprising first conclusions and consider them as possibilities, provided that we also have the courage to correct these deductions should new points of view arise. In short, we must leave ourselves completely open to all possibilities."[2]

Continued efforts to devise a means of opening the two rolls proved unproductive, however. One professor suggested encasing each layer in a thin sheet of gold, which would provide a flexible backing for the brittle copper. Another professor suggested

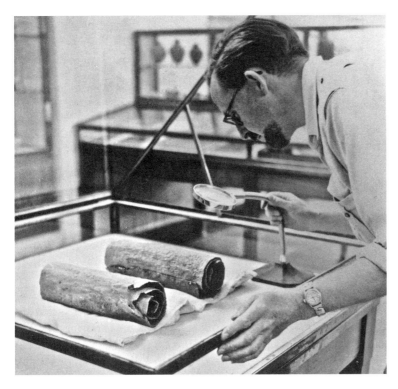

Hebrew letters could be read in reverse on the outside of the copper rolls from Cave 3. Here John Allegro examines the inscription, which had been hammered into the copper sheets before they were rolled up.

slipping a sheet of sensitized film between the layers. Experiments were conducted in the United States on replicas of the scrolls to see if some flexibility could be restored to the oxidized copper. But all efforts to devise a method of reconstituting the metal so that the scroll could be unrolled failed.[3] And with the passage of time, the two rolls were deteriorating further.

In 1954 Kuhn recommended cutting the layers of the rolls into longitudinal strips—a little like peeling off the layers of an onion—and, as part of the process, covering each successive layer with a plastic shield to prevent the metal from shattering in the process.

In 1955, with the two objects still rolled up three and a half years after they had been recovered, an English member of the scroll-publication team named John Marco Allegro convinced

John Marco Allegro was a young scholar on the scroll-publication team who convinced de Vaux to let him bring one of the copper rolls to England to see if it could be opened there. When Henry Wright Baker was ultimately successful in opening the roll, Allegro became the first scholar who could read Hebrew to see the text.

de Vaux and Harding to allow one of the rolls—the smaller one—to be brought to Manchester, where he lived, to see if experts there could create a method to unroll it.

In Manchester, Allegro had complete control of this roll. And this was to introduce a personal element into the story of the Copper Scroll that has all the intrigue, animosity and revenge of a murder mystery.

At the time Allegro suggested that the roll be brought to Manchester, he had no idea of what expertise was available there or whether anyone in Manchester would be interested in undertaking the task. (If you think this says something about Allegro, both good and bad, you are right.) As it turned out, Allegro did not have much luck interesting anyone in the project from the University of Manchester, where he had been teaching. In his own words, they treated him "curtly."[4]

He then approached the Carborundum Company Ltd of Trafford Park, a firm that specialized in manufacturing grinding

In order to open the scroll, each roll was placed on a spindle and secured there with dental plaster. The metal was then sprayed with a plastic adhesive to prevent the brittle copper from shattering at the touch of the spinning saw blade.

wheels. But that firm decided it lacked the machines necessary to undertake the task.

A colleague then suggested to Allegro that he try the Manchester College of Science and Technology. There he met Henry Wright Baker, a professor of mechanical engineering who described himself modestly to Allegro as a "mere plumber." Wright Baker later described his introduction to the matter:

> It was entirely through a chance conversation [with the president of the college, whom Allegro had contacted] in a local train that the writer was asked, as an engineer, if it was possible to cut pieces from old and brittle bronze, and gave his opinion that the cutting itself should present no special difficulty if fragmentation were prevented by the application to the exposed surfaces of one of the modern adhesives, which should form a tough and resilient backing having considerable powers of penetrating the interstices of the corroded material.[5]

This makes it sound easy. But as one observer has noted, "The opening of the Copper Scroll not only required technical

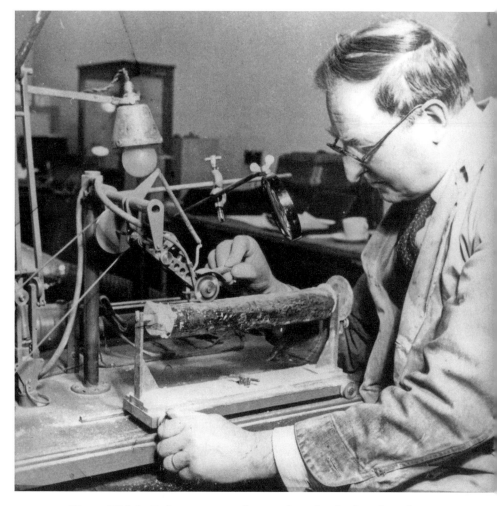

Henry Wright Baker was a professor of mechanical engineering at the Manchester College of Science and Technology whom Allegro approached about unrolling the Copper Scroll. Wright Baker adapted a thin, round saw to cut the copper roll into long, cupped strips. The copper roll moved along a track under the saw blade, which was lowered manually to make the cuts.

excellence but courage as well."[6] Wright Baker had both.

Wright Baker was in fact building on (or adopting) Kuhn's suggestion of cutting the layers of the roll into longitudinal strips, while covering each successive layer of metal with a plastic adhesive to prevent it from crumbling.

Wright Baker created a specially designed contraption to

undertake the operation. It looked as if it might have been designed by Rube Goldberg. It was made from British military equipment that had been de-accessed after World War II. Although it looked strange and unwieldy, it was in fact very well thought out.

A spindle was inserted through the hole in the center of the roll, which was then placed in a secure position on a cradle. The cradle was then mounted on a small trolley with metal tracks on which the cradle could run. Above the tracks, at the end of a spring-loaded arm, was a circular saw that could move up and down but was otherwise stationary. The roll, rather than the saw, did the moving. This electrically driven saw was about 1.75 inches in diameter and only 0.006 inches thick. It had been designed to saw the splits in pen nibs. Moving the cradle along the tracks would bring the roll under the saw blade, which could be lowered with a fingertip control. A magnifying glass set above the saw enabled the operator to control the depth of the cutting—which had to be limited to the one-millimeter depth of the oxidized copper layer.[7] Another tube would spray aircraft adhesive on the exposed skin of the roll to prevent it from shattering when the blade touched it. In this way, the roll could be cut into concave strips approximately 12 inches long.

When Allegro first saw the contraption, he had his doubts, especially because "when the motor was switched on, the whole machine jumped convulsively on its base every time the knot on the string connecting the motor to the saw ran over its pulley wheel."[8] Allegro reports that Wright Baker went ahead and made the first test cut without Allegro's being there: "In case the worst had happened and the precious document shattered into a thousand pieces as the saw touched the surface, he had wished to be alone in his misery."[9] In fact, the contraption worked beautifully, although that could hardly have been known in advance.

I fear that this description has over-simplified the process. It was in fact considerably more complex from beginning to end. For example, dry dental plaster was rammed around the axle to affix the roll to the spindle. A small fan-blower cleared the dust as the saw did its work. After the rolls had been cut into strips, the inner faces were washed with a special solution to seal the surfaces and prevent further corrosion. And on and on.[10]

In an effort to avoid destroying any of the letters in the course of the sawing, Wright Baker sought to place the cuts in the margins of the text. In many cases he was successful, although not always. He reports that, of the 3,000 letters in the Copper Scroll, only 2 percent of the letters that were there before he undertook to open the scroll were "doubtful" after he completed his work.[11] In order not to destroy letters, in two cases he decided not to make the cut in a straight line.

Gradually, Wright Baker became practiced in the art of cutting the rolls, reducing the cutting time from ten minutes to two-and-a-half minutes per cut. The entire operation on the first roll took little more than a week.

With word of Wright Baker's success, the larger roll was brought to Manchester, where it, too, was soon cut into longitudinal strips by the same process as the smaller roll. The result was a total of

When the roll was finally cut open, the writing on the inside was fully revealed for the first time (pictured here with Allegro's facsimile). Scholars in Jerusalem were initially dependent on Allegro's facsimile because even photographs were not clear enough to read the letters.

After the first copper roll had been successfully unrolled, the second roll was also sent to Manchester. The two rolls were cut into a total of 23 cupped metal strips, each measuring approximately 12 inches long, containing a total of 12 columns of text.

23 segments of concave strips, which is still how the Copper Scroll exists today.

At this point in the process, the entire document could be studied for the first time. It had originally consisted of three separate sheets, about a millimeter thick, that had been riveted together. In the rolling process two thousand years ago, one of the sheets broke off at the rivet line, creating two separate documents, one twice as long as the other. Each sheet was just short of 12 inches (30 cm) high and 31 inches (80 cm) wide. Including all three sheets, the Copper Scroll was nearly 8 feet long and was inscribed with a total of 12 columns of text.

Even though the content of the scroll was completely exposed, it was no simple matter to read it. Wright Baker described the process of identifying each letter as "very tedious." Creases and irregularities in the copper sheet distracted the eye. The writing was on a curved surface, making it especially hard to see. The letters had been punched out while the copper sheet had rested on a relatively soft surface (probably wood) so that the punch could push the letters out. They extruded on the back only the same distance as the thickness of the copper sheet (about 0.03 inches). Some lines of writing extended over two and sometimes three of the 23 segments.

The metalworker who created the letters was probably illiterate (perhaps this was a security measure). He was simply given a text to follow, but he could not read it. Moreover, the text was probably inscribed on the copper sheets by more than one metalworker, perhaps as many as four. Each letter usually required more than one blow of the hammer on the punch. The workmen had available only a limited number of metal punches, insufficient for all the curves and subtleties needed for accurate rendering of the Hebrew letters. As a result, some of the letters are incomplete.

Moreover, the fine distinctions between different Hebrew letters are not always preserved in this hammered script. Thus, it is often difficult, if not impossible, to distinguish between two different letters on the basis of the hammered script alone. For example, *waw* (*vov*) is simply a longer vertical line than *yod*, but in this text the difference is not clear by simply looking at the letter. Only the context provides a key to identifying the correct letter. It is often similarly impossible, by looking only at the hammered letter, to see any difference between *dalet* and *resh* or *bet* and *kaph*, letters that bear small distinctions in Hebrew script formed with a pen. And the orthography (spelling) of the text is not always what it should be. In Hebrew some letters are shaped differently when they appear within a word from when they appear at the end of the word. The Copper Scroll scribe(s) often confused a "medial" for a "final" letter. And the space between words is not always clear; the text is written in what scholars call *scripta continua*.

The lines of the text are often not straight. When a line was begun too high, it had to bend sharply downward to avoid the line above. Toward the end of the text (and sometimes at the

The writing on the scroll is often crude and uneven. In the last column (a replica of which is shown here), the scribe seemed to be worried about running out of space, so he cramped the letters together and then had more than enough room to spare at the end.

end of a column), it appears that the workman was afraid of running out of space, so he crowded the letters and made them smaller. Then it became obvious that some of this was unnecessary and he had space to spare at the end. Letters vary widely in size. The largest letters are as much as five times the size of the smallest letters. The writing looks "rough and unpracticed," in the words of one scholar.[12] "The man authorized to make [it] was no great expert of the art."[13]

Another difficulty for the scroll team: With the available camera equipment, photographs of the scroll were not clear enough to read the script. Even in the ultimate 1962 official publication of the Copper Scroll in Volume III of *Discoveries in the Judaean Desert*, the text of the script cannot be read from the photographs—both because of the curvature of the object and because the letters are indistinguishable from the oxidized and corroded copper. Because nothing but illegible photographs were available to transmit the text, a scholar either had to look at and study the scroll itself or depend on a hand-drawn facsimile. Three people transcribed the text early on from the scroll itself: Wright Baker; Muhanna Durra, a Jordanian artist who worked with Allegro; and Józef Milik (after the segments were sent back to Jerusalem), to whom publication of the Copper Scroll would officially be assigned. These transcriptions vary considerably, however. Wright Baker was hampered by the fact that he did not know Hebrew. The copy by Muhanna Durra and Allegro was revised by Milik based on his examination of the scroll itself. But discrepancies remained.

Despite these difficulties in reading the text of the Copper Scroll, one thing was pellucid: It described enormous amounts of buried treasure at over 60 sites that were described with varying degrees of precision. This simply confirmed what Kuhn had earlier concluded from his study of the outside of the rolls. Public, as well as scholarly, interest was mounting. Everyone, it seemed, wanted to know more.

Publication of the Copper Scroll proved not to be a simple matter, however. Added to the difficulties described above was something else that made it worse: warring personalities, chiefly those of Allegro and Milik (and de Vaux and Harding, as well). While official publication of the text was assigned to Milik (perhaps the most brilliant decipherer on the publication team), Allegro was the first person who could read Hebrew to see the opened scroll, in Wright Baker's laboratory in Manchester. And thereby hangs my tale.

CHAPTER 3

Squabbling Scholars

The relationship between John Allegro and the other members of the publication team was complex and wide-ranging. It involved a number of issues. As regards the Copper Scroll, the publication of its contents was one of those issues. Allegro, ever the publicist, wanted to tell the world. Milik, to whom publication was assigned, would not be rushed. He would follow usual scholarly procedures and produce a volume in his good time that all members of the publication team could be proud of. The other members of the team agreed with Milik. They were also committed to the scholarly tradition that no one but the assigned scholar had any "rights" to publish anything about the assigned text, certainly not on the basis of what he had learned as a member of the team, and certainly not simply as the emissary to Manchester who had overseen the unrolling of the scroll. But the fact is that Allegro was the first scholar with a knowledge of Hebrew to see the text. And it was his duty to transmit the text to Jerusalem by means of a hand-drawn copy (facsimile) of the text. So he had to understand it.

When the chief editor of the publication team, Father Roland de Vaux, assigned the publication of the Copper Scroll to Józef Milik, rather than to Allegro, Allegro says he was not offended. He, too, recognized Milik as "perhaps the most brilliant of our little team ... Milik was certainly the best fitted to carry the initial decipherment of the Copper Scroll a stage further, and since he had been one of the party that had ... found the scroll, it was doubly fitting that he should be entrusted with its edition for the definitive publication. I hoped that this would not be long delayed."[1]

Allegro's complaint in the end was that the official publication was, to his mind, inexcusably delayed. In fact it was not published until 1962, seven years after Wright Baker had opened the scroll in late 1955 and early 1956.

Allegro's daughter, Judith Ann Brown, has written a loving, respectful but honest biography of her father, including a description of his many warts. She accurately subtitled the book, "The Maverick of the Dead Sea Scrolls." John Strugnell, a member of the scroll-publication team, called Allegro "the stone in the soup." Frank Cross, another colleague on the team, described him as "a friendly and engaging person, but he was bent ... [he was] amoral—one of the few amoral people I have known."[2]

Allegro had been trained as a Methodist preacher. His contact with sophisticated biblical scholarship, however, ultimately led to a loss of faith. In his studies he was a brilliant and clearly rising star. So when Britain's leading Hebrew scholar, Sir Godfrey Driver of Oxford, was asked for a recommendation for an Englishman to join the scroll-publication team, Driver recommended his young Ph.D. student.

Allegro was the only atheist on the scroll-publication team. Most of the other members of the team were or had been Catholic priests (except for Cross and Strugnell—the latter would later convert to Catholicism—and a German scholar, Claus-

Hunno Hunzinger, who was on the team only for a very brief period). Nevertheless, at the outset Allegro seemed to get along fine. He was especially respectful of Milik, a Polish priest who later married and moved to Paris. Cross has called Milik "the most gifted member of the team ... He had the hands of hundreds of scribes in his head."[3]

The irreparable breach between Allegro and the rest of the team occurred in January 1956, just days after the arrival of the second roll in Manchester. Allegro, always eager to present his views to the general public, gave three talks on BBC local radio about the still little-known contents of the Dead Sea Scrolls. In these talks Allegro reported that the Wicked Priest described in the scrolls had delivered the leader of the Essene community at Qumran, known as the Teacher of Righteousness, into the hands of Gentile (read Roman) troops "to be crucified." Allegro continued:

> When the Jewish king had left and peace descended once more on Qumran, the scattered community returned and took down the broken body of their Master, to stand guard over it until the Judgment Day. For they believed that the terrible events of their time were surely heralding the Visitation of God Himself ... In that glorious day, they believed their Master would rise again, and lead his faithful flock, the people of the New Testament, as they called themselves, to a new and purified Jerusalem.[4]

In his third talk Allegro drew the parallel more explicitly:

> Last week, I said that the leader of this monastic community by the Dead Sea was persecuted and probably crucified by Gentiles at the instigation of a wicked priest of the Jews. For most of us, these events will associate themselves automatically with the betrayal and crucifixion of another Master, living nearly a century later.

The BBC talks by a member of the publication team with supposed access to the unpublished manuscripts created a media storm. *The New York Times* reported that "The origin of some Christian rituals and doctrines can be seen in the documents of an extremist Jewish sect that existed for more than 100 years before the birth of Jesus Christ." Even *Time* magazine reported on Allegro's BBC broadcast.

The other members of the publication team were furious. They strongly disagreed with Allegro's interpretation of the scrolls and their alleged connection to Christianity. Allegro, on the other hand, believed his colleagues were fearful of exposing texts to the public that could be seen as undermining Christianity. But equally important to the rest of the team was the fact that Allegro was discussing the content of the scrolls in a public forum before the scholars had finished with their basic study of them.

Scholarly convention gives (or gave—it is not clear to what extent this convention still exists) absolute control of a manuscript to the scholar who has been assigned publication of that manuscript. Whether any other scholar is permitted to see it is up to the assigned scholar. When the manuscript will be published and under what conditions are also up to the assigned scholar. No other scholar may publicly discuss the contents of the manuscript until it has been officially published by the assigned scholar. If the assigned scholar grows elderly or becomes ill without publishing the manuscript, the assigned scholar may reassign it or bequeath it to another scholar—at least, so the convention was interpreted at the time. Moreover, only students of the assigned scholar are permitted to study it—and even then only to aid, of course, the assigned scholar's effort to publish it. Allegro described this convention as characterized by "a fierce regard for appropriated rights ... that is redolent of the jungle."[5]

At the very time that the Copper Scroll was being unrolled (or cut up) in Manchester and its publication assigned to Milik, Allegro was giving his BBC talks. The second of the two rolls (the larger one) arrived in Manchester within a few weeks of the broadcasts. No one else—not even Milik—had seen the contents of the Copper Scroll. Some of the members of the team thought that Allegro's talks had something to do with what he had learned from reading the Copper Scroll. If that had been the case, it would have been an unpardonable breach of scholarly etiquette. The suspicion that this may have happened only added to the fury at Allegro's radio talks by his colleagues on the team.

Allegro maintained that his assertion concerning crucifixion was based on his study of the Dead Sea document known as the Nahum Pesher, which had been assigned to him for publication. According to Allegro's interpretation of that text, it states that the leader of the Dead Sea Scroll sect, the Teacher of Righteousness, was crucified and was expected to rise again. Indeed, the Nahum Pesher does refer to "a man hanged alive on [the] tree," the common Hebrew locution for crucifixion.

De Vaux, on the other hand, suspected Allegro of basing his references to crucifixion on the Copper Scroll, whose publication had been assigned to Milik. In a letter to de Vaux, Allegro hotly denied this accusation. But in the same letter, he refers to the fact that the reference to crucifixion in the Nahum Pesher had "confirmation" in the first column of the Copper Scroll in a passage that Allegro had translated as "the sepulcher of ... the Crucified [One]."[6] The publication team continued to believe that Allegro had improperly used his advance look at the text of the Copper Scroll.

Equally, if not more, offensive were Allegro's assertions that the Dead Sea Scroll community was the precursor, or even direct predecessor, of Christianity. The relationship of the scrolls to Christian origins is still a sensitive, if not controversial, matter.

As early as 1949 the French epigraphist André Dupont-Sommer began publishing his views on the then-available Dead Sea Scrolls, seeking to draw a direct line from the Dead Sea Scroll community, generally thought to be a Jewish sect known as the Essenes, to Christianity. In Dupont-Sommer's view, the

French epigraphist André Dupont-Sommer published his view early on that there was a direct connection from the Teacher of Righteousness of the Dead Sea Scrolls to Jesus of Nazareth.

Teacher of Righteousness was martyred and identified as the messianic "savior of the world."

In a now-famous passage, Dupont-Sommer wrote:

> The Galilean Master ... appears in many respects as an astounding reincarnation of [the Teacher of Righteousness in the scrolls]. Like the latter He preached penitence, poverty, humility, love of one's neighbor, chastity. Like him, He prescribed the observance of the Law of Moses, the whole Law but the Law finished and perfected, thanks to His own revelations. Like him, He was the Elect and the Messiah of God, the Messiah redeemer of the world. Like him, He was the object of the hostility of the priests ... Like him he was condemned and put to death. Like him He pronounced judgment on Jerusalem, which was taken and destroyed by the Romans for

having put Him to death. Like him, at the end of time, He will be the supreme judge. Like him He founded a Church whose adherents fervently awaited his glorious return.[7]

Dupont-Sommer greatly influenced the prominent American literary critic Edmund Wilson, who wrote a best-selling book on the scrolls, reprinted from a series of articles that appeared in *The New Yorker* from 1951 to 1954.[8] Wilson, following Dupont-Sommer, claimed that the Qumran sect and early Christianity were "successive phases of a [single] movement."[9] Wilson drew out the implications of Dupont-Sommer's position:

> The monastery [at Qumran], this structure of stone that endures between the bitter waters and precipitous cliffs, with its oven and its inkwells, its mill and its cesspool, its constellations of sacred fonts and the unadorned graves of its dead, is perhaps, more than Bethlehem or Nazareth, the cradle of Christianity.[10]

Dupont-Sommer and Wilson have been heavily criticized by the academic community—but on the basis of a subtlety that escapes many laypersons. It is generally agreed today by virtually all scholars that there is no direct relationship between the Dead Sea Scroll community (Essenes, if that's what they were) and Christians or Christianity. On the other hand, it is also very widely agreed that Christianity grew out of the same Jewish soil represented by the Dead Sea Scrolls. This is a subtle but important distinction. Many of the ideas of the Dead Sea Scroll sectarians were later to appear in early Christian thinking. The Dead Sea Scroll sectarians believed in a messiah— actually two of them—who would come at the end of time and redeem them. One Dead Sea Scroll fragment explicitly states: "Son of God he will be called. And Son of the Most High they will call him" (4Q246—The Aramaic Apocalypse). Compare this with Luke 1:32–35: "He will be great and will be called the

Edmund Wilson, an American literary critic who was greatly influenced by Dupont-Sommer's views about the scrolls, wrote a series of articles for The New Yorker *in the 1950s that called the Qumran sect and Christianity "successive phases of a [single] movement."*

Son of the Most High ... Of his kingdom there will be no end ... He will be called the Son of God."

Other Dead Sea Scrolls seem to prefigure the Beatitudes in the Gospels. The most popular books of the Hebrew Bible found at Qumran (fully a quarter of the 900 different Dead Sea Scrolls are biblical manuscripts) are also the books of the Hebrew Bible most frequently quoted in the New Testament (Psalms, Isaiah and Deuteronomy). This list of similarities could be substantially extended. Some scholars even believe that John the Baptist spent his early years at Qumran. (Few, if any, suggest that Jesus lived at Qumran, although he may have visited; he was baptized by John the Baptist nearby in the Jordan River, and the traditional Mount of Temptation is a mere stone's throw from Qumran.)

The point is that there are many similarities between early Christian thought and the views reflected in the Dead Sea Scrolls—and the latter preceded the former by at least a hundred years. All scholars agree on this. On the other hand, there are also some important differences between the Dead Sea Scroll community and early Christians. The Qumranites believed in extreme purity rules and strict adherence to intricate, often formalistic laws that distinguish it from the Christian community and its doctrines.

The Dead Sea Scroll fragment known as The Aramaic Apocalypse (4Q246) refers to a messiah who will be called "Son of God." This is one example of language that was used both by the Dead Sea Scroll community and by early Christians, indicating their common (but distinct) origins. Both grew out of late Second Temple period Judaism.

In hindsight and in this context, it may seem difficult to understand why the members of the scroll-publication team got so seethingly upset at Allegro's BBC radio broadcasts, but they did. They decided to write a letter to *The Times* of London, disassociating themselves from Allegro. On March 16, 1956, a letter signed by de Vaux, Milik, Strugnell, Patrick Skehan and Jean Starcky appeared in *The Times*, repudiating Allegro and his BBC broadcasts:

> It has come to our attention that considerable controversy is being caused by certain broadcast statements of Mr. John Allegro, of the University of Manchester, concerning the Dead Sea Scrolls. We refer particularly to such statements as imply that in these scrolls a close connection is to be found between a supposed crucifixion of the "teacher of

righteousness" of the Essene sect and the Crucifixion and the Resurrection of Jesus Christ. The announced opinion of Mr. Allegro might seem to have special weight, since he is one of the group of scholars engaged in editing yet-unpublished writings from Qumran.

In view of the broad repercussions of his statements, and the fact that the materials on which they are based are not yet available to the public, we, his colleagues, feel obliged to make the following statement. There are no unpublished texts at the disposal of Mr. Allegro other than those of which the originals are at present in the Palestine Archaeological Museum where we are working. Upon the appearance in the press of citations from Mr. Allegro's broadcasts we have reviewed all the pertinent materials, published and unpublished. We are unable to see in the texts the "findings" of Mr. Allegro.

We find no crucifixion of the "teacher," no deposition from the cross, and no "broken body of their Master" to be stood guard over until Judgment Day. Therefore there is no "well-defined Essenic pattern into which Jesus of Nazareth fits," as Mr. Allegro is alleged in one report to have said. It is our conviction that either he has misread the texts or he has built up a chain of conjectures which the materials do not support.

The letter had the opposite effect from that intended by its authors—as any marketing consultant could have predicted. Allegro was now even more famous. Requests for interviews and lectures poured in. He had more media access than ever to circulate his views.

But he was reviled by his colleagues on the scroll-publication team. And it was in this context that much of the animosity over the publication of the contents of the Copper Scroll played out.

CHAPTER 4

Publication Rights— and Wrongs

A t the time John Allegro made his BBC broadcasts, no public announcement had yet been made of the contents of the Copper Scroll, even though the media were aware of, and duly reported on, Wright Baker's efforts to open the rolls. Allegro could hardly restrain himself: Some public announcement should be made, he felt.

Six weeks after the scroll had been opened in Manchester, *The New York Times* reported that "Professor [Wright] Baker said he believed not a letter [of the text] had been lost." The public pressure to reveal some sense of the contents was obviously building. But Allegro played by the rules, much as he chafed. He dutifully and promptly transmitted his facsimile drawing of the text of the Copper Scroll (made in collaboration with Muhanna Durra), as well as his notes, to the director of the Department of Antiquities, G. Lankester Harding, in Jerusalem.

(His transmittal was never even acknowledged.) Moreover, he kept his mouth shut, despite the press's increasing interest. At this time, he was still playing by the rules.

Another issue at this time divided Allegro from his colleagues: He believed that the buried treasure described in the Copper Scroll was *real!* Other members of the team regarded it as folklore, a typical ancient legend.

When an official announcement on the opening of the rolls was finally released in Amman on June 1, 1956, it disclosed that indeed the Copper Scroll described the "hiding place of ancient treasure, altogether about sixty hoards ... consist[ing] of gold and silver."[1] But it characterized the hoards of treasure as "a collection of traditions ... The total amount of gold and silver listed amounts to nearly 200 tons, obviously a fantastic figure, and coupled with the depth at which some of the hoards are alleged to lie—16 to 18 feet—makes one doubt the authenticity of the stories."

Some observers have speculated that the scholars concluded that the list of treasure was fictitious not because they really believed it, but rather because of their fear that the announcement of real treasure would lead to a flood in the desert: a flood of treasure seekers turning the place upside down in search of the loot, which in turn would mean the destruction of an enormous number of ancient sites. As Cross wrote to Allegro, "No one wants all our antiquities sites dug into confusion."[2] Allegro himself was aware of this danger and early on was committed to secrecy: "One whisper that there's real treasure awaiting the digger at Qumran, and the Bedu would be down there in a flash and turn the whole joint upside down," he wrote to Harding.[3]

But there were other aspects of the June 1 announcement that angered Allegro. The release mentioned the "ingenuity and patience" of Professor Wright Baker and his assistant in opening the scroll, but failed to make any mention of Allegro, who had overseen the entire project. To add insult to injury, the release noted that the text had been "studied and a preliminary translation made by Abbe [Józef] Milik" in Jerusalem.

Gerald Lankester Harding (at right) was the British head of the Jordanian Department of Antiquities, which controlled most of the Dead Sea Scrolls until 1967. He is pictured here with Roland de Vaux (left) and Józef Milik (center) at the Qumran excavation in the early 1950s, which Harding co-directed with de Vaux.

Perhaps understandably, Allegro was furious. "My participation has been denied, and no credit has come to me for advising on every cut made, or reading and forwarding the transcriptions and translations," Allegro bitterly wrote to Harding.[4]

The depth of the animosity on both sides at this point is perhaps best revealed in connection with a lecture that was given by Wright Baker at the John Rylands Library in Manchester, in which he described his opening of the scroll.[5] According to Allegro, the Jerusalem authorities "sternly warned me to keep away [from Wright Baker's lecture] lest I should be pressed [by the media] for information on the contents [of the scroll]."[6] In his lecture, Wright Baker minutely and meticulously described how he had opened the scroll, but failed even to mention Allegro or his connection with the project. He, too, must have been instructed by "the Jerusalem authorities."

Moreover, as time went on it appears that Allegro was indeed miffed that the publication of the Copper Scroll had been assigned to Milik, instead of to him. In a letter to Frank Cross, Allegro wrote:

> If you take my tip you'll get just as much stuff out as you can a.s.a.p. In lay quarters it is firmly believed that the Roman Church in de Vaux and Co. are intent on suppressing this material. Nonsense we know, but this business of holding back important documents [like the Copper Scroll] merely to boost a particular publication lends itself to such fantasies. Furthermore, the fact that it [the Copper Scroll] was lifted right out of my hands to be placed firmly in those of a Roman priest [Milik] who already has enough on his plate for a decade has had its effect, despite my urging that in taking on the job of opening, I laid no claim to publication of the results.[7]

This letter thus exposes another issue: Allegro's colleagues felt that the atheist Allegro was propagating the idea that the Vatican was suppressing release of the Dead Sea Scrolls generally because these ancient documents allegedly somehow undermined Christianity, a claim that had no validity at all: Neither the Vatican, nor any other Catholic authority, had made (nor made thereafter) any effort to suppress publication of the scrolls. As Allegro's letter to Cross reflects, Allegro was not himself disseminating the idea at this time, although he later came to this erroneous view.

As early as 1954, Allegro began writing his first book on the scrolls. It was published in 1956 as *The Dead Sea Scrolls*.[8] Ever the publicist and marketer, he would have liked to have treated the story of the Copper Scroll in the book, but he held back, deferring to academic tradition that he could not deal with the text until it had been officially published by the scholar assigned to it.

When it came to the second edition of his book, Allegro was again faced with the question of discussing the Copper

Allegro's public statements about unpublished scrolls and his controversial views about their content caused a rift between him and the rest of the publication team. He became impatient with the delay in Milik's publication of the Copper Scroll and published his own book about it in 1960.

Scroll. In a letter to a colleague that reflects both his cupidity and impatience regarding this restriction on describing the contents of the Copper Scroll, Allegro wrote that he could "sell another million [copies of my book] if I could [mention the Copper Scroll]."[9] But again he held his hand.[10]

The Dead Sea Scrolls is a chatty, personal, informal account designed to appeal to the general public. Fully aware of the personal aggrandizement of the book, Allegro also believed passionately in letting the masses into the scholar's study. He truly wanted to keep the public informed, in contrast to the more cautious scholarly attitude of waiting for a clearer picture when a more confident scenario could be shared with a wider public.

By 1957 Allegro had completed a book manuscript (in association with David Noel Freedman, a leading American biblical scholar) that would ultimately become *The Treasure of the Copper Scroll*, but he deferred publishing it. He scheduled it for a 1960 publication on the assumption that Milik's official version of the Copper Scroll would be out by then. In a letter to a colleague, he wrote that he hoped to "get some sort of clearance" to publish his book. "But the main point," he went on, "is: When is Milik intending to publish the official version? ... We [Freedman and I] don't want to jump the gate. At least, that's not strictly honest; I'd love to jump the gate, but think it wiser not to."[11]

Milik's first publication concerning the Copper Scroll had

been in 1956 in a semi-popular magazine of the American Schools of Oriental Research.[12] He mentions Wright Baker's successful opening of the scroll and even the individuals who actually transported the two rolls from Jerusalem to Manchester. But there was no mention of Allegro. Milik also repeats his contention concerning the fictional nature of the buried treasure and engages in some strange speculation to account for his view that this simple list of treasure without the usual folkloristic narrative framework has no basis in historical reality:

> It goes almost without saying that the document is not an historical record of actual treasures buried in antiquity. The characteristics of the document itself, not to mention the fabulous quantity of precious metal recorded in it, place it firmly in the genre of folklore. The Copper Document is thus best understood as a summary of popular traditions circulating among the folk of Judaea, put down by a semi-literate scribe. He was, no doubt, one of the group of hermits who lived in caves nearby Khirbet Qumran ... It is a private effort, highly individual in character and execution, perhaps the work of a crank.

Of the actual text, Milik, almost teasingly, provides the reader with an English translation of 4 of the 64 caches of treasure.

Year after year, Milik continued to publish articles on one narrow aspect or vague broad aspect of the Copper Scroll without publishing the actual text. In 1957 Milik published his own *Ten Years of Discovery in the Wilderness of Judaea* (*Dix ans de Devouvertes dans le Desert de Juda*). Unless I am mistaken, it includes only two sentences about the Copper Scroll (quoted here from the English edition, published in 1959):

> Further, the archaeologists unexpectedly discovered a third cave containing manuscripts, two of which were rolls of copper. The text was engraved on them in Hebrew

A brilliant scholar, Father Jozef Milik was assigned thousands of scroll fragments from Cave 4 to publish, as well as the Copper Scroll. His overwhelming workload led to long delays in the publication of his assigned texts. In 1962, seven years after the Copper Scroll was opened by Wright Baker, Milik finally published the editio princeps *of the scroll.*

square letters, a few of which could be read in relief on the back of the rolled strips of metal.

In an article published in that same year (1957), Milik released the Hebrew text of the four sites for which he had previously given English translations, but no more.[13]

In 1959 in French[14] and in 1960 in English, Milik published articles giving his *translation* of the Hebrew text of the Copper Scroll (before or simultaneously with publication of Allegro's *The Treasure of the Copper Scroll*, discussed below), but these articles do not provide other scholars with the Hebrew text or with photographs. "The reproductions (photographs and facsimiles) and the complete [Hebrew] transcription of the text, together with an extensive commentary, must be reserved for the *editio princeps*," Milik wrote.[15] In this article he also continued to assert that the scroll describes "purely imaginary treasures belonging to Jewish folklore of the Roman period."

Whether it was this publication by Milik of a translation of the Hebrew text that led Allegro to feel justified in going ahead with his own book containing his facsimile drawing of the text as well as his translation,[16] or whether he was simply so tired of waiting for the official publication and disgusted with what he regarded as an overly restrictive scholarly convention is not clear. In any event, when Milik's official publication did not appear, Allegro went ahead with the publication of *The Treasure of the Copper Scroll* in 1960 containing both his facsimile drawing of the text of the scroll and his translation.[17]

Finally, in 1962, Milik's *editio princeps* of the Copper Scroll was published by the Oxford University Press in volume 3 of *Discoveries in the Judaean Desert of Jordan.*[18]

Allegro has often been accused of "pirating" or "stealing" the Copper Scroll from Milik.[19] As Welsh scholar Philip Davies has observed, however, "A dispassionate observer can perhaps see both sides of the matter (and indeed so could Allegro), but my own sympathies are with Allegro here."[20]

Moreover, Allegro also claims that, after G. Lankester Harding was discharged by the Jordanians as director of the Jordanian Department of Antiquities in 1956, the new director gave him (Allegro) "full rights to make my own publication of the text, denying vehemently that Milik or any of the museum personnel had permission to do so."[21] Allegro was obviously on very good terms with the Jordanians. He dedicated *The Treasure of the Copper Scroll* "by gracious permission" to "His Majesty King Hussein." In 1961 Allegro was appointed Scroll Advisor to His Majesty's Government.

CHAPTER 5

Folklore or Temple Treasure?

Is the buried treasure described in the Copper Scroll at 64 locations real or just folklore?

Almost all scholars today believe the Copper Scroll describes real buried treasure, contrary to the view of Milik and the official scroll team. As one scholar has said, "No writer could fail so exceedingly if the intent had been to produce a romance of hidden, glorious temple treasure. We read nothing of a golden menorah ... much less of an ark of the covenant—those items which would have been highlighted if this were a folktale as Milik proposed."[1]

The one prominent remaining holdout is Harvard's Frank Cross.[2] Cross found Allegro's view that the treasure was real "quite bewildering." Cross noted the "vulgar dialect in which it is written," "the clumsiness of the scribe," "the often vague or traditional places of concealment" and finally stated: "I am dubious that even the temple of Herod could have mustered such glittering heaps of gold and silver, much less that such amounts escaped the greedy besiegers." While these quotations are quite old, I talked to Cross more recently about the matter; he continues to be of the same opinion. He called the text "the mad dreams of some ancient; the engraving was done by an illiterate."[3]

He then asked me if I was convinced that the treasure was real. I replied: "Unlike many scholars, Frank, I have room in my heart for uncertainty."

"Ah, good, good, good," he replied.

"So many scholars out there think they've got *the* answer. Just as every archaeologist thinks that his excavation, just by happenstance, has the key to everything." We both laughed.

"Yup," he conceded—and then added, with regard to the excavation site he is associated with, "Ashkelon *does*." Again, we both laughed.

The truth is, while I do have a modicum of uncertainty about the reality of the Copper Scroll treasure, it is not as persistent as I may have expressed to Cross, in deference to his magisterial stature. Yes, I have my doubts, as you will learn at the end of this chapter, but they are comparatively minor.

The Copper Scroll consists of a simple list. It is not attributed to an ancient hero like Moses or Jeremiah or even a priest. It has absolutely no narrative framework. It is not part of a story, real or fictional. It is composed in a dry, concise, factual style—almost as if it were written by an accountant—listing one hoard of treasure after another until more than 60 hoards are documented. To characterize its style as merely prosaic is to exaggerate its literary quality.

Each of the caches follows a certain order of description. As Al Wolters has described it, "In an unvarying pattern, the 64 sections present material in the following order: (1) a designation of a hiding place; (2) a further specification of the hiding place; (3) a command to dig or measure; (4) a distance expressed in cubits; (5) a treasure description; (6) additional comments."[4]

No description contains all of these elements, but whatever elements each description does contain are in this order.

Here are a few examples of the caches described in the Copper Scroll, hardly the stuff of folklore:

> In the funerary shrine, in the third course of stones: 100 gold ingots.
>
> In the large pit that is within the court of the peristyle, in the gutter of its bottom, sealed in the entrenchment opposite the upper door: 900 talents.
>
> Between the two chambers that are in the Valley of Achor, midway between them, dig 3 cubits: two pots are there, filled with silver.

That's all—no story, no hero, no setting. Just the facts. As P. Kyle McCarter of The Johns Hopkins University has observed:

> It is extremely difficult to imagine that anyone would have gone to the trouble to prepare a costly sheet of pure copper and imprint it with such an extensive and sober list of locations unless he had been entrusted with hiding a real and immensely valuable treasure and wanted to make a record of his work that could withstand the ravages of time.[5]

It is not only that copper was especially valuable in ancient times or that it cost more than animal skin or papyrus. The use of copper was chosen to indicate that the contents were of special significance: The information on this scroll was important enough to record on copper. Pure copper would hardly be used to record mere folklore.

This is the only copper scroll among the more than 900 Dead Sea Scrolls. It is also the only autograph (an original manuscript, not a copy) among the scrolls.

That it is no easy task to inscribe a text on copper is a strong indication of the text's significance. To prepare this scroll, it was not simply a matter of getting some ink and a scribe. On the contrary, each letter had to be hammered in, one at a time. As one scholar has written, "Hammering letters into expensive copper sheets is time-consuming, noisy, costly and difficult to correct or update ... Parchment does not need relatively large-sized characters, as does copper sheet."[6]

The fact that the Copper Scroll is one of the longest metal inscriptions ever discovered also suggests that this is no fairy tale.

In Roman-period Egypt, temple inventories were written on copper.[7] An example from Medinet Habu offers a striking parallel to the Copper Scroll. Inventories from a Temple of Apollo on the island of Delos provide other examples. These analogous documents also provide hints as to the probable source of the treasure the Copper Scroll is describing (i.e., the Temple in Jerusalem).

Roman military diplomas, so-called *diplomata militaria*, granting citizenship to foreign veterans of the army, were usually written on copper,[8] which simply emphasizes the point that only important inscriptions were written on copper.

The last paragraph of the Copper Scroll gives the location of "a duplicate of this document and an explication and their measurements and a detailed inventory of everything, one by one." In other words, this copy of the referenced treasures was intended to be cryptic, as if it were an abstract of a master copy. Some scholars have called it an *aide-memoire*. One scholar suggests that it was "for people already familiar with the whereabouts of most of the hiding places."[9] Another scholar has called it a "summarizing inventory list."[10]

What about the vast amounts of treasure described in the Copper Scroll? Isn't that a clear indication that the treasure is just a legend without factual basis?

Milik made the argument, "The characteristics of the document itself, not to mention the fabulous quantity of precious metals and treasures recorded in it, place it firmly in the genre of folklore."[11]

Only the most important documents, such as this Roman diplomata militaria, were deemed worthy of being inscribed on copper. These so-called military diplomas granted citizenship to 25-year foreign veterans of the Roman auxiliary forces or praetorian fleets. This example comes from the Roman province of Syria-Palaestina.

But just how large is the treasure described in the Copper Scroll?

The official announcement in Amman of the opening of the scroll said that the amount of gold and silver was "nearly 200 tons." In an early article, Milik changes that to "more than 200 tons."[12]

Judah Lefkovits, who wrote his doctoral dissertation on the Copper Scroll, reduces the amount of precious metals in the caches to less than 60 tons. Moreover, he says, less than 17 percent of this is gold, the rest being silver and unspecified metal that could be copper or other metals.[13] If this figure is correct, the total amount of buried gold would be approximately 10 tons—not so outlandish a figure.

It is difficult for me to check these figures for a number of reasons, aside from my indolence. The amount of gold is sometimes expressed in "ingots" (Locations 2, 7). How much did an ingot weigh at the turn of the era? Or how much did the silver in a "chest" weigh (Location 1)? How much did the silver in a "jar" weigh (Locations 11, 32)?

When the reference is to talents, it is often not specified whether the metal is gold, silver or perhaps copper; in other words, just the number of talents is given (Locations 3, 6, 10, etc.). When a metal *is* specified, it is almost always silver, not gold.

When the number of talents of gold is specified, it is usually a reasonable number, such as two (Location 34) or five (Location 58).

The only large amount of gold is in Location 49, which indicates a cache of "300 talents of gold." One scholar, however, translates the passage as "300 talents of silver coins, gold coins,"[14] so it could be either. Still another distinguished translator indicates his hesitation by noting that there is a space before the word "gold," as if letters are missing.[15] So it is not even certain that "300 talents of gold" is the correct reading. In any event, the "fabulous" amount of gold essentially hinges on the reading of this one cache. But let us assume, as does seem likely, that it refers to 300 talents of gold.* How much is that? How much does a talent weigh?

The word for talent originated as the load a man could carry. Later, it was the weight of an oxhide-shaped copper ingot. At other times it was the weight of 3,000 *shekels*, or 60 *minas*. In short, no one is sure just how much a talent weighs. Estimates vary from 60 to 300 *minas*, whatever that weighed. In pounds, the most common guesstimate is that a talent in ancient Israel weighed somewhere between 66 and 76 pounds;[16] others suggest

---

*A question has been raised as to whether the Copper Scroll is even referring to talents. The Hebrew word for talent (*kkr*) is often abbreviated as *kk* in the Copper Scroll, but is this in fact an abbreviation of talent? Lefkovits also questions whether this abbreviation should be read *kk* or perhaps as *kb* or *bk* or *bb* since, as noted earlier, the Hebrew letters *bet* and *kaph* are difficult to distinguish from each other on the Copper Scroll, in which case it would not be an abbreviation for talent. See Judah K. Lefkovits, *The Copper Scroll (3Q15): A Reevaluation* (Leiden & Boston: Brill) pp. 472–473, 479.

Due to the similarity of the Hebrew letters bet *and* kaph *(the two high-lighted letters on the right in this drawing are* bets; *the one on the left is a* kaph*), as well as the crude writing on the Copper Scroll, it is unclear whether the abbreviation usually read as* kk *refers to talents (*kkr*) or to something else.*

50 or even 25 pounds.[17] But it is not always clear whether these guesstimates apply to the time period when the Copper Scroll was written—what scholars call the late Second Temple period. (On paleographical grounds, Frank Cross dates the script to between 25 and 75 A.D.)

Milik estimates the weight of a talent at about 75 pounds. So let's take his figure. Assuming the single large cache of gold describes 300 talents of gold, this would come to about 22,500 pounds, or a little more than 11 tons. Is this an outlandish amount?

Greek sources tell us that Alexander the Great found about 1,200 tons of precious metal when he conquered Susa—a far cry from the 11 tons of gold in the Copper Scroll. In all of Persia, Alexander found more than 6,000 tons (more than 600 times as much as the Copper Scroll cache of gold).[18]

Antiochus IV Epiphanes carried off 1,800 talents from the Jerusalem Temple when he sacked it in 164 B.C.[19] (At 75 pounds a talent, this would come to 135,000 pounds or 67.5 tons.) The first-century Jewish historian Josephus reports that even after Pompey had plundered the treasury of the Temple in 63 B.C., Crassus discovered another 2,000 talents of silver (150,000 pounds, or 75 tons). The gold Herod used in the construction of the sanctuary on the Temple Mount equaled 8,000 talents (600,000 pounds or 300 tons).[20]

We know from the Arch of Titus in Rome that the Romans found much treasure in the Temple when they destroyed it in 70 A.D., including the menorah and the showbread table. Great amounts of gold must also have been housed in the Temple treasury, which functioned as a kind of priestly bank. Josephus notes that so much gold came on the market at the fall of the Temple that the price of gold in Syria dropped by half.[21]

Considering all this, we may regard the cache of 300 talents of gold referred to in one location in the Copper Scroll as not unreasonable and, in any event, an anomaly among the 64 caches.

If the amount of the treasure is not so outlandish as to be fictional, whose treasure was it? And where did it come from?

For Milik, it belonged to the residents of Qumran—rather, for him, that was where the story was made up. In his view the Copper Scroll was "no doubt [composed by] one of the group of hermits who lived in caves near Khirbet Qumran, and presumably was associated with the Essene community."[22] These hermits,

according to Milik, would hardly have these large amounts of treasure.

A variety of suggestions have been put on the scholarly table, but the most widely accepted view is that the Copper Scroll describes buried treasure from the Temple in Jerusalem.

The amount of the treasure may not be so

The Arch of Titus was erected over the Via Sacra in Rome to commemorate Titus's conquest of Judea in 70 A.D.

This relief on the Arch of Titus depicts spoils from the Temple being carried off after Jerusalem was captured by the Romans. In addition to the menorah and showbread table (shown here), the Temple treasury must have contained large amounts of gold and other precious items. Was it all captured by the Romans, or is some of it buried treasure listed on the Copper Scroll?

large as to be outlandish, but it is large enough to exclude every other suggestion except the Temple (and remember the text is written in Hebrew).

Another factor also points to the Temple treasury as the source of the caches described in the Copper Scroll. The buried items include artifacts that are almost certainly from the Temple. For example, in Location 4 the buried treasure includes what Kyle McCarter calls "vessels of contribution with a lagin and ephods," that is, items owing to or belonging to the priests.

The translation of Oxford's Geza Vermes says the cache includes "ephods (priestly garments)" and "the offering" of the "second tithe."[23] Florentino Garcia Martinez's widely used translation translates the same words as "tithe vessels of the lord of the peoples and sacred vestments."[24] Another authoritative translation (by Michael O. Wise) has "votive vessels—all of them flasks—and high-priestly garmenture," as well as "second tithe."[25] Other translations differ somewhat,* but all agree that the cache refers to cultic paraphernalia.

Other caches also refer to cultic items. Locations 8 and 9 refer to vessels that McCarter believes are sacred vessels. Location 13 includes "sprinkling bowls, chalices, libation bowls, ewers." Location 59 includes "oil flasks." Location 43 includes "sacrificial silver." Location 15 includes "vessels of contribution," which apparently were vessels into which tithes or other Temple contributions were deposited. Similar vessels are included in Location 62. Location 57 includes "liquid contribution, (that is,) disqualified contribution."

Apparently the buried treasure also included a book (scroll) that could take its importance only from the fact that it was a sacred book (Location 27).

Although the function of many of these items is not always clear and sometimes we are not even sure exactly what they are, it does seem clear that they have a religious denotation and are related to the Temple.

Another reference is especially intriguing. Location 32 reads as follows: "In the cave that is next to the cooling place belonging to the house of Hakkoz, dig 6 cubits: six jars of silver." Some of this text is difficult to read, but "the house of Hakkoz" is absolutely clear. Hakkoz was the name of a priestly family that

---

* The translation I generally use in this book is from the as-yet unpublished commentary of Professor P. Kyle McCarter of The Johns Hopkins University prepared for the Dead Sea Scrolls commentary series of The Princeton Theological Seminary Dead Sea Scrolls Project. McCarter initially used new high-resolution photographs of the scroll taken in 1991 by Bruce and Kenneth Zuckerman of the West Semitic Research Project. McCarter's text has since been updated somewhat on the basis of new readings provided by the recent digitization and conservation of the scroll by the Électricité de France (EDF) (see Chapter 8). Professor McCarter's entire English translation of the text of the Copper Scroll appears in the appendix of this book. I am extremely grateful to Professor McCarter for making this unpublished translation available in this way and to Professor Charlesworth for allowing me to publish this translation that will appear in the Princeton series.

traced its ancestry to the time of David (1 Chronicles 21:4).[26]This gives a singular reality to the treasure.

Finally, a number of the locations of buried treasure appear to be in the neighborhood of the Temple. More on this in the next chapter.

At a symposium on the Copper Scroll held at the University of Manchester in 1996, a straw poll taken of the assembled experts indicated that a majority thought that the treasure was real and probably came from the Jerusalem Temple.

The only alternative source of the treasure, though remote, is the Essenes, assuming that the settlement at Qumran was home to a community of these ascetics.[27] But it is hard to imagine that the Essenes would have had a treasury of these proportions.

Although it seems that the Copper Scroll describes real treasure that came from the Jerusalem Temple, a number of mysteries still surround the text. One, which all agree is unsolved, is the Greek letters in the text. Seven of the early descriptions of caches (Locations 1, 4, 6, 7, 10, 14 and 17) end with two or three Greek letters.[28] What in the world are Greek letters doing in a Hebrew text that is supposedly written at the direction of Temple authorities? Why are they noted in these early caches and not others?

The forced suggestions that the Greek letters are code letters to identify certain vessels or to identify different parts of the Temple budget or to represent secret numbers or abbreviations for personal names are all unsatisfying and, in the end, unsatisfactory.[29] It is easy to agree with Judah Lefkovits: "The significance and mystery of the Greek letters in the Scroll may remain unsolved." Al Wolters called them an "enigma."[30] Józef Milik regarded them as simply "inexplicable."

Other questions also remain unanswered. Why are the directions to the buried treasure so vague and uncertain? The explanation that this is only an *aide-memoire* for people who know the exact spot where the treasure is buried is really not very satisfying.

Why would something so important be engraved so poorly,

Seven listings near the beginning of the Copper Scroll end with Greek letters. The first one ends with the letters ΚεΝ, seen at the left end of the fourth line. No one has yet discovered what these Greek letters in the Copper Scroll mean or what they are doing in a Hebrew inscription.

with spelling errors and unclear letters? This is especially true toward the end of the document. As one epigraphist has observed, "The attention of the copyist petered out or his time was short and he had to hurry to finish."[31] The writing becomes cramped and crowded at the end, as if the scribe feared running out of space. Maybe the engraver was illiterate and was chosen for security purposes, so he would not be able to read the text.

How was this so-called scroll stored in the Temple? It could not be rolled and unrolled like a Torah scroll written on parchment. And it is almost 8 feet long. It is tempting to say that it was a plaque affixed to a wall. But there are no indications on the back of the scroll that it was attached to anything. As Wright Baker observed, "If used as an ornamental wall plaque, one would expect nail holes to be visible along one end at least. Yet none could be seen." And it would make no sense to tack up a secret document on the wall.

Perhaps it was initially rolled up (and broke at the rivet line between the second and third plaques) with the thought it could be laboriously unrolled after the crisis had passed.

How did the copper rolls get to Cave 3 at Qumran? That it was discovered in a cave with animal-skin scrolls associated with Qumran has led some commentators (both Milik and, ultimately, Allegro) to associate the Copper Scroll with the Dead Sea Scroll community at Qumran. The Temple authorities were the bitter opponents of the sectarians responsible for the other Dead Sea Scrolls. If the Copper Scroll was deposited independently of the Dead Sea Scroll sectarians, how did the Temple authorities find this spot to deposit the scroll?

When was the Copper Scroll deposited in Cave 3? The obvious suggestion is that it was deposited here just before the Roman conquest of Jerusalem in 70 A.D. But, on second thought, this creates a problem: The Romans had already conquered the Jericho area (including Qumran) in 68 A.D. Certainly the Temple authorities would not deposit the key to their treasures in an area already conquered by the Romans. With this consideration, it has been suggested that the Temple authorities deposited the scroll before 68. But was it so obvious at that time that Jerusalem was liable to be conquered by the Romans and that the Temple treasures should be hidden? Perhaps so: The Jewish revolt had already begun in 66 A.D. Or perhaps as the Romans approached Jerusalem after 68, the area around the Dead Sea was devoid of troops and it was safe to come there to hide the Copper Scroll—at least that was the chance the Temple authorities decided to take when they chose this cave to hide the scroll. However, there was probably a settlement of Roman troops camped at Qumran.

So while it seems clear that the Copper Scroll is describing real treasure that probably came from the Jerusalem Temple, many questions remain.

CHAPTER 6

Locating the Treasure

C an we locate the caches of treasure described in the Copper Scroll? It is clear that many of them are located in and around Jerusalem and in the area of Qumran.

Some sites are described more specifically than others. Often a site with a more specific geographic location is followed by other caches with little or no indication of the geographic location. It seems that the sites without specific locations are located in the same general area as the cache more specifically described in an earlier listing.

For example, Location 57 states that the treasure is "in the place of the two reservoirs," in the reservoir. The following three caches are apparently also "in the place of the two reservoirs," although they do not say so. Location 58 is quite detailed, but without specifying the more general geographic location. The cache is buried "at the western entrance [...] of the mausoleum, (where there is) an overflow duct." But where? Location

59 simply asserts that the treasure is "under the black stone." The same for Location 60: "Under the threshold of the crypt." Presumably, all these caches are located "in the place of the two reservoirs," as referred to in Location 57.

We find this same pattern in the area around Qumran: Location 1 states (in most translations) that the treasure is buried in the ruins of "the Valley of Achor, beneath the steps that enter to the east." The cache in Location 2 is simply "in the funerary shrine, in the third course of stones," presumably in the same ruins in the Valley of Achor where the first cache is located. The cache in Location 3 is "in the large pit that is within the court of the peristyle, in the gutter of its bottom, sealed in the entrenchment opposite the upper door." Again we assume that this cache is in the ruins of the Valley of Achor, as specified in Location 1.

Sometimes the principal location is explicit—"the Valley of Achor"—and sometimes the location must be deduced. For example, Location 30 refers to the "ford of the high priest," suggesting we might be in the vicinity of the Temple. Location 31 speaks only of an "aqueduct." As we know, two aqueducts from the south brought water to the Temple Mount, so we can guess that Location 31 is also in Jerusalem, perhaps on the Temple Mount itself, where the aqueducts ended.

Location 32 locates treasure at the house of Hakkoz. We have already noted that the house of Hakkoz was a well-known priestly family whose ancestry traces back to King David and is mentioned in the Bible. So we can deduce that Location 32 is also in the Jerusalem area.

Location 39 refers to Shaveh. After Abraham defeats Chedorlaomer in Genesis 14:17–18, Melchizedek, king of Salem (Jerusalem) and priest of God Most High, comes out with bread and wine to bless Abraham in the Valley of Shaveh, so this, too, must be some place near Jersualem.

Location 48 locates a treasure at the "reservoir of Beth ha-Kerem." In the Bible, Beth ha-Kerem is the home of the chief of the clan that repaired Jerusalem's Dung Gate when

Location 50 of the Copper Scroll specifically mentions "Absalom's Monument." This monumental tomb in Jerusalem, known today as Absalom's Tomb, has nothing to do with King David's son, but it is most likely the site referred to in the Copper Scroll.

the Jews returned from the Babylonian Exile (Nehemiah 3:14). That same Beth ha-Kerem is also mentioned in one of the Dead Sea Scrolls (the Genesis Apocryphon). Israeli archaeologist Yohanan Aharoni has identified it as the site of Ramat Raḥel, just south of Jerusalem. (Beth ha-Kerem is also the name of a modern suburb of Jerusalem, but this has nothing to do with the ancient site.) In any event, it is clear that Location 48 is in the Jerusalem area.

The most specific location in the entire scroll may be Location 50, which refers to Absalom's Monument. The well-known Absalom's Tomb, in the Kidron Valley below the Temple Mount, is as impressive today as it was when the Copper Scroll was engraved (although it is clearly not the tomb of David's wayward son Absalom). It is possible that a different tomb, rather than the one in the Kidron Valley, was called Absalom's Monument 2,000 years ago, but this seems highly unlikely, especially since the present Absalom's Tomb dates to the Hellenistic period, hundreds of years before the Copper Scroll was engraved. The cache at this location, the scroll tells us quite specifically, is hidden under the monument on the western side.

The site of Location 53 is almost as specific but harder to identify: What appears to be Temple paraphernalia ("vessels of discarded contribution" and "an accounting") is buried "under the southern corner of the portico, in the tomb of Zadok under the column of the exedra." Location 54 also refers to the "tomb of Zadok." It describes "consecrated material" buried "in front of the courtyard of [the tomb of] Zadok under the large cover which is at its base." Zadok was the original high priest under David and Solomon (2 Samuel 8:17; 1 Kings 1:8,34–39). His descendants were known as Zadokites. No doubt many Temple priests were later called Zadok. Other Zadoks are also mentioned in the Bible. Zadok's Tomb probably refers to one of the Kidron Valley tombs adjacent to Absalom's Tomb. One of these elaborate tombs may well have been called Zadok's Tomb at the time the Copper Scroll was inscribed. This suggestion is supported by the fact that two of these tombs do seem to fit the description in the Copper Scroll: Both look west. Both have columns. One even has a columned portico. Both have what might be described as a courtyard. In later times, one of these tombs was known as the Tomb of James the Just, Jesus' brother. In Hebrew, he would have been known

These tombs in the Kidron Valley are known today as (from left to far right) Absalom's Tomb, the Tomb of Bene Hezir, the Tomb of Zechariah, and Jehoshaphat's Tomb, but it's possible that when the Copper Scroll was written, one of them was called Zadok's Tomb, where the caches in Locations 53 and 54 are buried.

as Ya'akov (James) ha-Zadok (the Just One). So it might well have been known as the Tomb of Zadok at the turn of the era.

Today, the Kidron Valley tombs adjacent to Absalom's Tomb are known as the Tomb of Zechariah and the Tomb of Bene Hezir. A Bible dictionary I consulted lists 32 people in the Bible named Zechariah, including a prophet whose book is included among the so-called Minor Prophets, as well as the father of John the Baptist (Luke 1). The name probably refers to an attributed Zechariah, rather than to one of the real Zechariahs, in the same way that Absalom's Tomb is falsely attributed to Absalom. The attribution of the Tomb of Bene Hezir has more claim to historical reality; it is based on a difficult-to-see inscription scratched on the tomb, but this may not have been visible at the turn of the era, and the tomb may have

Along the eastern wall of Herod's Temple Mount stood Solomon's Portico, seen here at upper left, opposite the entrance to the Temple. At the upper right is part of the Royal Stoa, in this model by Leen Ritmeyer. Allegro considered the possibility that Solomon's Portico was referred to in Location 53.

been attributed to Zadok. Still another candidate for Zadok's Tomb is a tomb at the end of the line of these Kidron Valley tombs, known as Jehoshaphat's Tomb, another false attribution. The bottom line is that the tombs adjacent to Absalom's Tomb are enticing candidates for Zadok's Tomb as referred to in the Copper Scroll. Allegro refers to the Tomb of Bene Hezir as St. James's Tomb.[1] He identifies Zadok's Tomb as the southernmost tomb.[2]

But it appears that Allegro also considered another possibility for Zadok's Tomb, based on the description in Location 53, "under the southern corner of the portico ... under the column of the exedra." Along the ancient eastern wall of the Temple Mount was a long columned portico known as Solomon's Portico. Jesus taught in the Portico of Solomon (John 10:23), and the apostles congregated here: "They were all together in

Solomon's Portico" (Acts 5:12; see also Acts 3:11). At the southern end of this portico, at the southeast corner of the Temple Mount, is the Pinnacle, the point on the Temple Mount with the longest drop to the ground below. It was from here that the devil tempted Jesus: "If you are the Son of God, throw yourself down from here" (Luke 4:9; Matthew 4:5). (Jesus refused, saying: "You shall not tempt the Lord your God.")

On the southern end of the Temple Mount was a large basilica with an apse. When the Romans conquered Jerusalem in 70 A.D., they destroyed this many-columned basilica, and many of the pieces fell to the ground below the southern wall of the Temple Mount. They were excavated by Benjamin Mazar in the 1970s. Orit Peleg, a doctoral student at The Hebrew University, is writing her dissertation on these fragments of the basilica. Part of this structure may be the "exedra" referred to in Location 53 of the Copper Scroll.

Allegro thought that Zadok's Tomb might well be at the base of the Pinnacle, at the southeast corner of the Temple Mount. Whether or not any of these sites is the Tomb of Zadok referred to in the Copper Scroll, it is clear that

The southeastern corner of the Temple Mount is known as the Pinnacle because it is the spot from which the drop to the ground below is greatest. Allegro thought that Zadok's Tomb, as referred to in the Copper Scroll, might be located at the base of the Temple Mount here, "under the southern corner" of Solomon's Portico.

it refers to a site in Jerusalem near the Temple Mount.

The two caches in the Copper Scroll following the references to the Tomb of Zadok (Locations 55 and 56) are almost without a description as to their location. In their entirety they read:

> In the grave that is under the bushes: 40 talents.

> In the grave of the common people—it is clean. In it are vessels of contribution or spoiled contribution, with an accounting alongside them.

The intention, apparently, is that these locations come under the rubric described earlier, that is, the Tomb of Zadok. All four caches are somewhere in the vicinity of the Tomb of Zadok in the Kidron Valley below the Temple Mount.

Allegro desperately wanted to dig for treasure in Jerusalem. More specifically, he wanted to look under the surface of the Temple Mount itself. It had not been explored since the 1860s, when Charles Warren and Charles Wilson worked there on behalf of the London-based Palestine Exploration Society. They had explored more than 40 underground cisterns, cavities, vaults and tunnels. Allegro was sure there was much more to learn, especially because two locations of the Copper Scroll in the Jerusalem area involved aqueducts that may be the ones that led to the Temple Mount. Allegro speculated that as many as "two dozen of the scroll's locations are situated within the Temple area ... Only persons having an intimate knowledge of the Temple courts and their chambers, their private names and functions, would be able to recognize them and rob them of their sacred treasure."[3]

The Jordanian Minister of Education, in his capacity as Head of the Dome of the Rock, issued a permit for Allegro's projected work on the Temple Mount, but the chief of the Haram esh-Sharif (the "Noble Sanctuary," as the Temple Mount is known in Arabic) felt that he could not deliver it without the approval of the man whom Allegro called "the Muhaffiz, the

Several of the Copper Scroll locations seem to cluster around the Jerusalem area, especially the Temple Mount, giving weight to the theory that the buried treasure came from the Jewish Temple. Allegro wanted to look beneath the Temple Mount and almost received permission from the Muslim authorities, but in the end he was denied a permit.

big cheese of Jerusalem." The Muhaffiz said that he himself approved of Allegro's excavation plans, but he first would have to consult the military. Allegro then walked the Temple Mount with the appropriate brigadier in the hope and expectation that he would approve the project. But in the end, the army opposed the project.

"Why, nobody seems to know," Allegro wrote to his wife. "It's not a military area, except insofar as Jerusalem is one." Allegro suspected it was the influence of his erstwhile colleagues on the scroll-publication team.[4] For him, this suspicion was confirmed by Roland de Vaux's scathing review in the journal of the École Biblique of Allegro's Copper Scroll book.[5] Allegro's team, de Vaux asserted, was "prevented at the last

Allegro identified the Copper Scroll's reference to Zadok's Tomb as the southernmost of the Kidron Valley tombs, which is known today as Jehoshaphat's Tomb. He led an excavation at this tomb but failed to find any treasure.

moment from extending their depredations to the esplanade of the Mosque of Omar [i.e., the Temple Mount]."

But Allegro did excavate at the Kidron Valley tombs that he regarded as Zadok's Tomb (Jehoshaphat's Tomb) and St. James's Tomb (the Tomb of Bene Hezir). At Zadok's Tomb, he found a low hidden wall that could have been an irrigation channel, but no treasure.

Although he did not dig at Absalom's Tomb, Allegro recalled a story about some girls from a nearby convent who had picnicked by the tomb in 1900. One of the girls found a hole that she climbed through and came out with her apron full of gold coins, which were confiscated by the nuns and never heard of again. In Allegro's biography, the author remarks that Allegro found "only the echo of the rumor" when he tried to learn more about the story.[6]

. . .

Even before he began his efforts to dig in Jerusalem, Allegro had explored the other area that he regarded as most promising: the area around Qumran.[7]

Location 61 describes a cache on Mount Gerizim, which is hardly in the Qumran area. It lies near Shechem (modern Nablus) about 30 miles north and west of Qumran. Mount Gerizim is well known from the Bible as the mountain where God will dispense his blessings on Israel; it stands opposite Mount Ebal, the mountain of the curses (Deuteronomy 11:26–30). At the turn of the era, when the Copper Scroll was engraved, Mount Gerizim was the holy mountain of the Samaritans, with whom the Jews were often in conflict. At first glance Mount Gerizim, located in Israel rather than Judah, seems a strange place to hide the Temple treasure—and in a totally different area from the other caches. But a closer look reveals that the Copper Scroll might be referring to another place altogether—one nearer Qumran. Sources from the first centuries of the common era consistently place Gerizim (and Ebal) near Jericho. Perhaps these sites were established, Kyle McCarter suggests, as part of an anti-Samaritan polemic.[8] Mt. Gerizim near Shechem is still the holy mountain of the Samaritans. But the Copper Scroll's Gerizim is probably an undetermined site near Jericho, which marks the northern limit of the sites of caches around Qumran.

Four locations (22, 23, 24 and 26) mention a place called Secacah. Location 26 is especially intriguing because it mentions two specific sites in addition to Secacah: The 32 unspecified talents buried 7 cubits underground are in the "Wadi Kippa on the way from Jericho to Secacah." Thus we begin to outline the area near Qumran where treasure was buried. The location of Jericho is, of

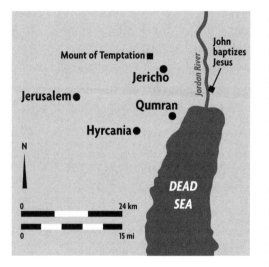

Even before exploring the sites around Jerusalem, Allegro considered the area around Qumran as the most promising for locating sites and caches mentioned in the Copper Scroll. Jericho marks the northern limit of these sites.

course, well known—about 7 miles north of Qumran. Secacah is mentioned in Joshua 15:61–62 as a town in the Desert District.

Allegro thought Secacah was Qumran itself—an identification many scholars still agree with. Others prefer other sites in this general location. Milik, Cross and McCarter identify Secacah as Samra, a small ruin in the plain known as the Buqei‘a, a few miles west of Qumran.

If Secacah was Qumran, it is difficult to imagine that Temple treasure would be secreted here, since the Qumran sectarians were opponents of the Temple authorities (and vice versa). Those scholars who favor the Secacah=Qumran identification therefore tend to conclude either that the treasure is fictional or was deposited in Cave 3 by someone other than the Temple authorities, especially the Essenes (that was Allegro's guess).

We have already referred to the first location in the list of caches in the Copper Scroll, which mentions the Valley of Achor. This may fix the other end of the area around Qumran where much of the treasure is buried. Location 1 reads as follows in McCarter's translation:

"In Harubah, which is in the Valley of Achor, beneath the steps that enter to the east, 40 lath cubits: a chest of silver and its vessels. Weight: 17 talents. KɛN"

The Valley of Achor figures in several places in the Bible, most prominently in the story of Achan in the Book of Joshua. After the Israelite destruction of Jericho, all the contents of the

The "Valley of Achor" is mentioned in the first location on the Copper Scroll, as well as numerous places in the Bible. While its exact location is uncertain, many scholars, including Allegro, have identified it with the Valley of Hyrcania, west of Qumran.

destroyed city were consecrated to the Lord—"proscribed" is the biblical word. Achan "took of that which was proscribed" (Joshua 7:1). God was angered and, as a result, the Israelites lost the first battle of 'Ai. When Achan was identified as the man who had taken the proscribed spoils and caused Israel to lose the battle, he and his whole family were brought to "the Valley of Achor." The text continues: "Joshua said, 'What calamity you have brought upon us. The Lord will bring calamity upon you this day.' And all Israel pelted him with stones. They put them to the fire and stoned them. They raised a huge mound of stones over him, which is still there. Then the Anger of the Lord subsided. That is why that place was named the Valley of Achor—as is still the case" (Joshua 7:24–26). Some scholars see a word-play between (the Valley of) Achor in the Copper Scroll and the biblical Achan.[9]

According to another biblical reference, the Valley of Achor runs on the northern border of Judah, near Jericho (Joshua 15:5–7).

The Valley of Achor also has eschatological resonances. At the end of time, in the words of the Prophet Isaiah,

My chosen ones shall take possession,
My servants shall dwell thereon.
Sharon shall become a pasture for flocks,
And the Valley of Achor a place for cattle to lie down.

Isaiah 65:9–10

Similarly in Hosea:

I will give her vineyards from there,
And the Valley of Achor as a plowland of hope.

Hosea 2:17 (English 2:15)

Scholars disagree as to the precise location of the Valley of Achor. Some identify it with the modern Buqei'a, the level basin—known today as the Valley of Hyrcania—that lies above the cliffs of Qumran to the west.

However, in the Roman period, the Valley of Achor was identified with another valley: According to the church fathers Eusebius and Jerome, the Valley of Achor is north of Jericho. It is this problem of geographical ambiguity that has led some scholars to denominate the Copper Scroll as an *aide-memoire*, a document to remind people who know the precise location of the treasure not to forget it. As one scholar has concluded, "The exact location of this valley is problematic."[10] Or, in another scholar's words: "One thing is clear: the Valley of Achor was in the vicinity of Jericho."[11]

McCarter capitalizes the first word in Location 1 as if "Harubah" were the proper name of some place. Many other translators have not done this. Moreover, McCarter tells us that he is not sure of the last Hebrew letter in the word: Is it a *heh* or

Khirbet Mird, or Hyrcania, is the site that Allegro identified as the "ruins" or "fortress" in the Valley of Achor described in Location 1. A palace that originally stood on the summit was probably built in the second century B.C. by the Hasmonean king John Hyrcanus and was later rebuilt by Herod the Great.

an *aleph*? Different scholars read it differently. Generally, however, the word is related to the Hebrew word for "ruins." In the opinion of almost all scholars, the treasure of Location 1 is to be found "in the *ruins* in the Valley of Achor." John Allegro, however, interpreted the Hebrew word as referring to a *fortress*. But he probably correctly identified the Valley of Achor (his identification of the valley was seconded by Milik, Cross and many others). The site Allegro marked as the location of the buried treasure was both a fortress and in ruins

· · ·

The ruins in the "Valley of Achor" that Allegro identified as Location 1 is known today as Khirbet Mird (the "ruins of Mird"). Originally, it was known as Hyrcania, presumably because the palace on top of this imposing desert summit was built by John

Hyrcanus, the Hasmonean king who ruled Judea in the late second century B.C. Hyrcania was later rebuilt by Herod the Great in the first century B.C., and at that time it formed one of a series of palace/fortresses that lined the Dead Sea and Jordan Valley, from Masada in the south to Alexandrium in the north. These palace/fortresses were intended to protect Herod's kingdom in case of an attack from the east by the Nabateans (and

The ruins of an ancient palace/fortress sit atop the summit of Hyrcania. The site probably went out of use when the Romans conquered the area in 68 A.D. It has never been professionally excavated.

they also provided a place of comfortable refuge for Herod in case his own people rebelled against him).

A major ancient road led directly from Qumran to Hyrcania,[12] which served as the main Judean military headquarters in the desert.[13] According to this scenario, the network of palace/fortresses in the valley to the east were early-warning stations, forward military and command posts designed to signal an impending attack.[14] When the Romans assumed direct control of Judea in 63 B.C., an attack by the Nabateans was no longer a threat, so these advance command centers were no longer needed.[15] Perhaps after Herod's death in 4 B.C., Hyrcania was abandoned. That would satisfy the first location's requirement—according to some scholars—that the site be in ruins.

Sometime in the Byzantine period (fourth–sixth centuries), long after Hyrcania had been destroyed and abandoned, the ruins were settled by Christian monks who transformed the place into a monastery. They built a prominent basilical church, some of whose mosaics are still *in situ*. Monastic cells abut a Herodian wall. Water was supplied to the site by two impressive plastered aqueducts that collected runoff water. The water from the infrequent desert rainstorms was collected in cisterns that pepper the site.

In the Byzantine period, the site was known as Castellion, Latin for "fortress." Its current name, Mird, is a corruption of the Aramaic word *marda*, which also means "fortress."

Whether the first word in Location 1 is "fortress" (as Allegro believed) or "ruins" (as other scholars believe), if this is the Valley of Achor (which is a reasonable suggestion), then Hyrcania might well be the site referred to in Location 1 of the Copper Scroll. Moreover, it is also a good guess that this is the site of the treasures mentioned in Location 2 ("in the funerary shrine, in the third course of stones") and Location 3 ("in the large pit that is within the court of the peristyle, in the gutter of its bottom, sealed in the entrenchment opposite the upper door"), which have no more general description as to the area where they are located.

In early 1960 Allegro set out to see if he could find buried treasure in the ruins of Hyrcania. Allegro was convinced that Hyrcania was the site where the first three caches of treasure were buried. He decided to organize an expedition to explore the site. Incidentally, the site has never been professionally excavated, only surveyed. To assure maximum publicity for the expedition, which explored other sites as well as Hyrcania, he enlisted the sponsorship of *London's Daily Mail*, which supplied a reporter to send daily dispatches back to England. Jordan's King Hussein was also drawn into the project. The Jordanian government supplied troops for protection and transport.

Allegro's archaeological expedition spent several days at Hyrcania. At one point they discovered a shaft that led to a set of steps down to an ancient well. Excitement mounted: Was this the site mentioned as "beneath the steps that enter to the east"? One of the members of the expedition was lowered by rope down inside the well. It was filled with bats, but they were apparently more afraid of the archaeologist than he was of them. The expedition, fortunately, had the latest metal-detecting equipment on loan from the Signals Research and Development Establishment, Christchurch. It was used on all the walls and floor, but nothing was found of the "chest of silver" (Location 1) or the "100 gold ingots" (Location 2) or the 900 talents of unspecified metal (Location 3).

The undaunted explorers continued the search, however, in the vaulted cisterns and the remains of the royal halls. Allegro's archaeological surveyor, G.R.H. Wright, followed two stretches of Herodian walls that apparently enclosed the site, with towers at the corners. They were not able to identify the eastern entrance, however, as referred to in Location 1 of the Copper Scroll.

Location 2 refers, in McCarter's current text, to a funerary shrine. Allegro understood this, not unreasonably, as a "sepulchral monument" (this is still the translation of Florentino Garcia Martinez). Allegro thought he could identify "a construction crowning the peak of a small promontory overlooking the plain ... Closer inspection shows it to be more monu-

Allegro's archaeological surveyor G.R.H. Wright examines a wall inside one of Hyrcania's cisterns.

mental in character ... another relic of Herodian times."[16] This could well be the funerary monument referred to in Location 2. If so, it would not have been difficult to identify the "third course of stones." Again the metal detector was brought up front and center. With baited breath, the members of the expedition waited for the clicking that would tell them metal had been located. But when they heard the clicking that they thought would reveal a hundred gold ingots, it was not gold at all. The rock in the hillside had a natural magnetism that set off the metal detector. This made it impossible to distinguish a "natural" response from a response from hidden treasure. The clicking was the same. Allegro considered, but decided against, demolishing the entire "monument" in the hope of finding the treasure.[17]

Finally, as Allegro's biographer described it, "a full investigation would have to be left for a more thorough and professional investigation ... With disappointment, in the end they had to leave Mird's story unspoken. They had found ... rubble-filled wells, cisterns and passageways—but no skeletons and no treasure. The place was full of secret possibilities but they remained secret."[18]

Why has no treasure been found? Is it perhaps because someone in ancient times found the document mentioned in Location 64, which contained more specific directions as to where the treasures were buried, and dug up all of the caches?[19]

Perhaps the Romans discovered it all after the Great Jewish Revolt. They would not have needed the Copper Scroll or the document buried in Location 64 to find it: They had other methods. Indeed, Josephus reports that a Temple treasurer named Phineas delivered to the Romans various Temple artifacts that had been secreted, no doubt delivered under torture.[20] Disclosure by torture is recorded in other Roman records. In 106 A.D., barely a generation after they had conquered and burned Jerusalem, the Romans conquered Dacia, a small kingdom about where Romania is today. The king at the time, one Decebalus, had buried his treasure. To ensure its secrecy, he first diverted a river and buried his treasure in the old river bed. Then he brought the river back to its original course, over the buried treasure. Next he killed the workers and other personnel responsible for the project. Then he committed suicide. The victorious Romans, however, captured a friend of the king's and tortured him until he revealed the location of the treasure.[21]

The Romans knew that the treasure of the Jerusalem Temple surely contained vast quantities of precious metals. As one scholar recently observed, "As always, the key to their recovery lay with the interrogation of prisoners."

But there were those who still believed the treasure of the Copper Scroll lies buried and undiscovered at Khirbet Mird. One of them is an American airline pilot named Bob Morgan.

CHAPTER 7

Tunnel Mystery

Although Allegro's efforts at Hyrcania failed, the site probably remains the best candidate for locating lost treasure from the Copper Scroll. Many people have searched for a wall with steps to the east, as specified in Location 1 in the Copper Scroll, but none has found it. Perhaps it was part of the buildings that existed in the Second Temple period but have since been destroyed. Others have taken clues from Locations 2 and 3 and applied them to Location 1 but again have been unsuccessful.

Because the remains had never been professionally excavated, Allegro asked his archaeological surveyor, G.R.H. ("Mick") Wright, to survey the site. In the course of his work, Wright discovered two mysterious tunnels near the base of the hill on which the palace/fortress/monastery had been built.[1]

One, with a larger passage, began about 6 feet above the valley floor. The tunnel was high enough to accommodate a 6-foot-tall person standing at full height and was nearly as wide.

It descended via steps! Could this be the steps referred to in the Copper Scroll? The second tunnel was similar, but was closer to the valley floor and only the first couple of steps had been cleared. The first tunnel, which descended at a 30-degree angle, had been cleared to about a hundred feet. Apparently, Allegro's team did some excavating at the end of the hundred-foot passage but soon gave up. As he observed: "To cut such tunnels must have been a most laborious task and would not have been attempted for fun. Even at the depth so far penetrated, the air is heavy and warm and to clear away the rubbish would need

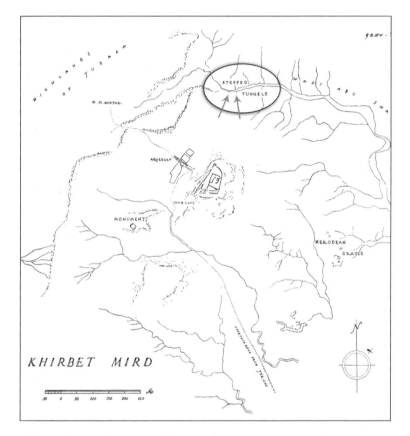

The ancient ruins of a palace and a monastery can be seen atop the mount of Hyrcania in this original site plan by G.R.H. Wright. Further north, at the foot of the hill, are two stepped tunnels that have intrigued scholars as the possible location of buried treasure or ancient tombs.

the provision of some form of forced air supply and a regular and frequent change of workers at the face."[2]

The tunnels remained a "mystery [that] tantalized our little expedition."[3]

In the early 1980s a Continental Airlines pilot named Bob Morgan (Charles Robert Morgan) from Kearney, Missouri, read these words, and he, too, was tantalized. Morgan had no archaeological experience but a great deal of determination. Describing himself as a devout Baptist, Morgan was mesmerized by the

During his expedition to Hyrcania, Allegro discovered a stepped tunnel at the base of the mount that he hoped was one of the locations mentioned in the Copper Scroll. However, after some exploration, the team came up empty-handed.

Dead Sea Scrolls. As a commercial airline pilot, he could go to Israel as easily as you or I could take a bus downtown. On vacations, he would go exploring for a couple weeks. From Qumran, he would wander by himself farther and farther into the desert, and eventually he came upon the site of Hyrcania. And of course he looked at the tunnels Allegro had written about. In the end, he decided to explore the tunnels. He began his excavation of the longer passage in October 1986.

He would dig alone or with a friend at night, using a simple little hand axe. As he said, it didn't matter whether it was night or day; it was always night in the tunnel. At night it was cooler and he wouldn't be disturbed by curious Bedouin—or the Israeli army.

Morgan is somewhat of a mystic. On one trip to Israel, he tried to contact Israel's most illustrious archaeologist Yigael Yadin, only to find that he had died prematurely at age 67 from a burst aneurysm. He also tried to contact John Allegro to find out more about his search for the treasures of the Copper Scroll, only to learn from Allegro's wife, Joan, that he, too, had died prematurely at age 65 from a burst aneurysm. He was struck by the parallel.

For years, Morgan read everything he could get his hands on about the scrolls. Finally, he began to weary of the scrolls and started reading literature about ancient Egypt. Again, he found some astounding parallels. "There is a very strong resemblance," he wrote, "between what is written in the Dead Sea Scrolls and the Egyptian religious beliefs at the ancient city of On [Heliopolis] during the Eighteenth Dynasty [c. 1569–1315 B.C.]."[4]

The first Hyrcania tunnel is aligned with the North Star. Morgan tells us that at night, from 300 feet down inside the tunnel, "the North Star is clearly visible in the center of the [tunnel] opening." Morgan noted that "alignment of the tunnel with the North Star is similar to the alignment of the ascending passageways in the great stone pyramids of Egypt ... This is a very good indication that whoever is responsible for the original excavation had Egyptian priestly knowledge." Could there be a

Decades after Allegro's expedition to Hyrcania, the mysterious tunnels at Khirbet Mird once again drew the interest of adventurers and scholars.

connection with Moses at the time of the Exodus? Bob wondered: Moses surely knew Egyptian culture. Was he responsible for the Egyptian connection at Hyrcania?

"Both the Egyptians and the Essenes [the authors of the scrolls] envisioned the sun setting atop the holy mountain," Bob observed, "and as the shadow of the mountain grew long, the souls of those buried in the valley entered and passed through the gate to ascend to heaven."

In the Damascus Document, fragmentary copies of which were found among the Dead Sea Scrolls, the Sabbath is said to begin "from the moment when the sun's orb is distant by its own fullness from the gate." While most scholars see this gate as the horizon, Morgan views it as an actual gate through which one would look to get the last sight of the sun.

Morgan thought this "probably correlates to the mountain at ancient Thebes in Egypt that overshadows the Valley of the Kings. The ancients referred to it as 'The Gate.'" In both civilizations, Morgan noted, "The sun is described as passing at the end of the day through a gate wherein it sinks." Moreover, the prophet Hosea also speaks of a gate[5]: "I will give her vineyards and make the Valley of Achor a gate of hope" (Hosea 2:15; Hosea 2:17 [Hebrew]).

Hyrcania, of course, lies in the Valley of Achor! As Morgan described it, "Mount Hyrcania is ... one of the tallest peaks [in the Judean Wilderness] and provides a commanding view across the Vale of Achor." With what he envisaged as putting two and two together, Morgan concluded that the gate of hope is in the Valley of Achor—at Hyrcania!

Morgan then began searching Jewish literature in the hope of finding a reference to the tunnel he had been exploring at Hyrcania. It was then that he stumbled on the fourth verse of the second chapter of 2 Maccabees in the collection of extra-biblical books known as the Apocrypha. There it tells of an oracle received by the prophet Jeremiah shortly before the Babylonian destruction of the Temple in which the prophet is told to take the "Tent [of Meeting] and the Ark [of the Covenant] ... to the mountain where Moses had gone up and had seen the inheritance of God." And Jeremiah did so, also taking with him "the altar of incense" from the Temple. When people tried to follow him, Jeremiah rebuked them:

> The place shall remain unknown until God gathers his people together again and shows his mercy. Then the Lord will disclose these things, and the glory of the Lord and the cloud will appear, as they were shown in the case of Moses.
>
> 2 Maccabees 2:4–8

Morgan believes Hyrcania is the mountain to which Jeremiah returned: Mt. Sinai. He thinks the tunnel itself goes back

Airline pilot Bob Morgan (left) was convinced that Hyrcania still held hidden possibilities. He eventually enlisted the help of archaeologist Oren Gutfeld (right) to continue excavation of the tunnel that Allegro had explored.

to the time of Moses, and that Moses himself is entombed somewhere at Hyrcania. He believes the tunnel is where the Ark of the Covenant may still lie hidden.

He has spent years excavating the tunnel. Through a charitable foundation that he created—the Liberty Historical Society—he has spent more than a hundred thousand dollars in his search of the tunnel.

At one point, Morgan decided it would no longer do to dig at night with a friend or two. He would try to associate with a professional archaeologist.

At first he had a difficult time making contact with a professional archaeologist. Bob was not a member of the academic community; he had no academic training. And he had been digging illegally—that is, without a permit. Finally, he managed to see Professor Amihai Mazar of The Hebrew University, who fobbed him off on one his graduate students, Oren Gutfeld.

Gutfeld told his story in an article in *Biblical Archaeology Review:*[6]

I was hardly in a position to say no. I was a mere graduate student. When Professor Amihai Mazar, the head of
the department of archaeology at The Hebrew University, asked me if I would talk to an American who wanted
someone to undertake an excavation, I, of course, said I
would be happy to see him. At the time, I was busy in one
of the laboratories of the Institute of Archaeology study-
ing a hoard of bronze artifacts that I had recently discovered in Tiberias on the Sea of Galilee. Into the laboratory
walked this tall man with a determined look in his eyes.
Dressed formally, he immediately spread open a map of
the Judean Desert. He told me that he knew of a "very
important" site in the region and wanted me to excavate
it with him.

At this point, he had not yet stated the name of the
site. But out came a stream of questionable facts and
vague locations, all related to a mysterious site in the
Judean Desert. He was hard to take seriously. We are
used to the "Jerusalem Syndrome" and its many varia-
tions. All kinds of people come to Jerusalem and are sud-
denly transfixed and transformed, infused with visions
and apocalyptic pretensions. This seemed to be one.
However, I finally agreed to go with him to the Judean
Desert to visit the site he wanted to excavate. When I
finally said "yes," he wanted to go immediately, at that
very instant. However, because the site was in a military
training area where soldiers were using live ammunition,
I insisted we wait until Friday morning, when no exer-
cises were to be conducted.

When we got there I was, frankly, astounded. There,
in the white limestone, was a carefully chiseled opening 6 feet high and 3 feet wide, with steps leading into

the darkness below. We entered the tunnel and carefully descended, using our flashlights to see where we were going. I noticed that along the sides at evenly spaced intervals near the top of the walls were ancient niches for oil lamps to provide illumination for the workers who dug the tunnel or possibly for subsequent visitors. The soot from the lamps was visible above the niches.

Gutfeld stands in the opening of the western tunnel at Hyrcania, which descends by steps for 328 feet into the earth. The purpose of the tunnel remains a mystery.

From the point where Allegro had stopped excavating the passage was only a small rabbit hole Bob had created by partially removing the fill. I asked how far this very small, very steep, unstable excavation extended. About another 50 feet, he said.

I was fearful of crawling any farther. Unlike the rest of the tunnel, which was carved from solid limestone, this excavation was through the sand and mud that had filled the tunnel over the centuries. The hole was so small that only one person would fit, and even then, there was no way to turn around to get out. When Bob said he wanted to go on, I told him I would meet him outside. Undeterred, Bob went to the end and brought back a sample.

When he returned with the sample, he asked me what I thought. Without hesitation, I replied, "Let's do it."

The Morgan/Gutfeld excavation (in his "preliminary report" of the excavation, Morgan describes Gutfeld as his assistant) began in April 2000, almost exactly 40 years after Allegro began exploring the tunnel in search of the treasure of the Copper Scroll.

Morgan and Gutfeld continued to dig farther into the tunnel, step by step, season after season, deeper and deeper. On one occasion Morgan was attacked by a knife-wielding Bedouin and had to be stitched up at a Jerusalem hospital, but he remained fearless. Their excavation permit was pulled by the army during the second Arab intifada (uprising), but they returned once it was over.

Allegro had managed to clear 62 steps, about 90 feet. Morgan dug an additional 90 feet (for a total of about 180) before he managed to link up with Gutfeld. Together they dug 100 feet beyond that. With the additional excavation by Gutfeld after Morgan left, the stepped tunnel was exposed for more than 300 feet beneath the mountain.

At about 150 feet the tunnel takes an abrupt bend to the

About 150 feet into the tunnel, it turns westward, creating a kind of doorpost that the team called the mezuzah. *Beyond this point the tunnel widens from 6 to 8 feet, but the reason is unknown.*

west, creating a kind of doorpost shortly beyond the bend. They took to calling this pseudo-doorpost the *mezuzah*, after the little box containing biblical verses often seen on the doorposts of Jewish homes. Beginning at the *mezuzah*, the tunnel gradually widened from about 6 feet to 8 feet. Why? they wondered. What was the significance of this? Were the excavators about to understand the purpose of the tunnel? Would they come upon buried treasure? Or would it be a tomb? Maybe even the tomb of Herod the Great? Thus were Gutfeld's dreams filled. And if these were Gutfeld's dreams, imagine Morgan's.

Complicating things still further, the tunnel forked. Which branch to follow—or both?

About 240 feet from the opening, Morgan maintains, a wall of small uncut stones blocked the tunnel and had to be removed. Gutfeld questions whether this was in fact a wall. What they do agree on is that shortly before the *mezuzah* (which Morgan says was preceded by this stone wall), they found the bones of a goat, scientifically identified as *Capra ibex*. Radiocarbon tests on the bones indicated that the goat died somewhere between 640 and 560 B.C. Morgan settles on 2,590 years before the present, or 590

B.C. Both Morgan and Gutfeld accept the radiocarbon results. Here their interpretations diverge.

Gutfeld is without an explanation. He believes the tunnel was probably dug in the Hasmonean period (second–mid-first century B.C.). So what are the bones of a goat who died in about 590 B.C. doing in the tunnel? Gutfeld has no explanation. He simply poses the question: "How in the world did the bones get there hundreds of years before we suppose the tunnel was dug?"

Morgan's scenario is different: Look at the date—590 B.C. Jerusalem was burned and the Solomonic Temple destroyed by the Babylonians in 586 B.C. Morgan believes these events— the destruction of the Temple and the deposition of the goat's bones in the tunnel—are not unconnected. For him something from the Temple was hidden somewhere behind that stone wall in the tunnel. The goat was an offering placed there, in front of the blocking wall to the inner sanctum of the tunnel. Study of the bones revealed no tooth marks that would have been there had a predator dragged a carcass into the tunnel. Even Gutfeld concedes that "the animal was buried there with his flesh intact." Morgan believes the tunnel was originally dug under Moses' supervision.

Gutfeld agrees that a few of the pottery sherds found in the tunnel were from the First Temple period. Only continued excavation would likely allow further interpretation.

According to Gutfeld, Morgan's interest in the project began to wane and Morgan himself became unreachable. Morgan says he could no longer financially support Gutfeld and his family. In any event, work on the tunnel stopped.

Then, in the fall of 2004, Gutfeld obtained a small grant from the Biblical Archaeology Society that enabled him to continue. Proceeding without Morgan, Gutfeld finally reached the end of the tunnel at 328 feet—a dead end. Nothing! Gutfeld has no explanation for the tunnel. He describes his unsuccessful effort at finding anything at the end of the first tunnel "one of the greatest disappointments" of his life.

Since then, Gutfeld has used GPR (ground-penetrating

Deep inside, the tunnel forks. In order to keep working, the archaeo-logical team devised a system by which fresh air was forced deep into the tunnel with hosing. They ultimately followed both branches to the end, but still they found no explanation for the tunnel.

radar) to determine whether there might be some cavities in the tunnel. Nothing came up. In the meantime, he has begun work on the second tunnel, 150 feet to the east. He does not give up easily. At this writing, he is 150 feet into the tunnel. Perhaps we will know more when he completes the excavation of the second Hyrcania tunnel.

Morgan still believes the Ark of the Covenant is buried somewhere in the tunnel.

No one, however, seems to know why the tunnels were dug. As Oren Gutfeld put it in his entry on Hyrcania in the soon-to-be-published supplement volume to the standard archaeological encyclopedia,[7] "The investigation of the tunnel has also not yet revealed its function; it has been suggested that it may have been part of a water system, a mine, a refuge [for rebels] or a tomb." Gutfeld has also suggested that it might have been make-work for prisoners sent here by Herod the Great. Or, conceivably, it was dug as a hiding place for Temple treasure hidden from the Romans, as described in the Copper Scroll.

Or maybe not.

CHAPTER 8

Saving the Copper Scroll

In 1994 it had been almost 40 years since Henry Wright Baker sawed open the Copper Scroll into 23 cupped strips at the Manchester College of Technology. The materials that had been used to consolidate and protect the scroll had aged. The cellulose nitrate glue that had been used in 1955 to hold the scroll together under the impact of the saw had yellowed, giving the scroll an unaesthetic appearance. Repeated handling of the segments had resulted in new breaks in the completely oxidized strips. Further damage resulted from the conditions under which the segments were stored and exhibited. Most important, new techniques had been developed to treat, preserve and protect the scroll for generations yet unborn.

This task was undertaken by the technological and scientific wing of the Électricité de France (the French Electric Company, or EDF).

Their first job was to remove the old surface adhesives and consolidate the fragments anew. But this was just the beginning of the project. Chemists would study all kinds of treating solutions for their suitability for preserving the scroll. The text would also be studied anew.

Metallurgists looked at the scroll with their electron microscopes and X-ray diffractometers. The text was examined applying spectrometry principles to the florescence of X-rays. Radiographical images were taken from several angles and then digitized, which flattened the curves and deformities in the letters, thus enabling the scientists, in cooperation with epigraphist Emile Puech at the École Biblique et Archéologique Française in Jerusalem, to restore previously unseen letters in the text. Sometimes fragments were reassembled differently from

Since their discovery and unrolling, the strips of the Copper Scroll have deteriorated further due to age, repeated handling and oxidation.

Here a scientist applies a protective layer of acrylic resin to one of the strips. In 1994 the French Electric Company (EDF) undertook the preservation of the Copper Scroll and the creation of a replica, using the latest technology.

Radiographical images, seen here, were taken of the strips from different angles and then digitized, enabling conservators to create flat, rather than curved, images of the text.

Flexible silicone was used to take a mold of each of the Copper Scroll segments. These molds were then joined to create a complete flat silicone mold of the Copper Scroll's three sheets. Here the mold is being removed from the silicone cast made of one sheet.

the previous assembly. All these processes resulted in improvements in the legibility of the document, revealing parts of the text that corrosive and damaging natural and human processes had made difficult, if not impossible, to see.

Almost as exciting was the creation of a flat reproduction of the 23 segments (not the originals, which retained their cupped shaped). Each of the segments was first molded with stretchable silicone. The negatives obtained in this way were then flattened, giving a reversed impression of the text of each of the

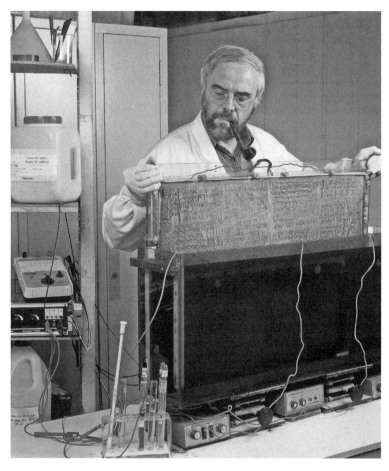

Once the silicone replicas had been created, the EDF scientists used a process called galvanoplasty to deposit a thin layer of copper over the entire surface. Here the created flat plaque (one of three) is being removed from its electrolysis bath.

segments. With these flat segments, each of the three original copper sheets that had been riveted together was recreated, and the three sheets were affixed to one another. Then a second reproduction in silicon was made from this negative, resulting in a positive image. The silicone sheet was then made conductive by a fine layer of graphite. Finally, by a process known as galvanoplasty (the deposit of metal by electrolysis), the scientists at EDF were able to create a flat reproduction of the entire scroll as it had looked some 2,000 years ago. At least five such

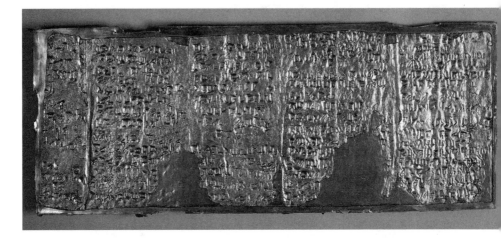

The new reproduction recreates the Copper Scroll as it looked before it was rolled up 2,000 years ago. Shown here is one of three similar plaques that were originally riveted together. At least five complete replicas were created and now reside at the Amman museum, EDF, the École Biblique and elsewhere.

reproductions were created—and at least one of them has disappeared. One is at the museum in Amman, another is at the École Biblique in Jerusalem and another at the EDF.[1]

As I write, the École Biblique's Emile Puech has just published a new translation of the Copper Scroll, together with a new commentary, based on the newly available materials from the EDF conservation of the Copper Scroll and the production of a flat replica.[2] Will this solve any of the mysteries that enshroud the scroll? Chances are it will raise as many new questions as it answers.

Text of the Scroll

This is a provisional translation of the Copper Scroll prepared by Professor P. Kyle McCarter for the Dead Sea Scroll commentary project of the Princeton Theological Seminary published by J.C.B. Mohr (Paul Siebeck) of Tubingen and may be improved on the basis of newly available studies and photographs. Copyright James H. Charlesworth, Director and Editor of the *PTS Dead Sea Scrolls Project*, 2007. Readers should check the version in that publication when it appears, together with a Hebrew text and commentary.

Location 1
In Harubah, which is in the Valley of Achor, beneath the steps that enter to the east, 40 lath cubits: a chest of silver and its vessels. Weight: 17 talents. KεN

Location 2
In the funerary shrine, in the third course of stones: 100 gold ingots.

Location 3
In the large pit that is within the court of the peristyle, in the gutter of its bottom, sealed in the entrenchment opposite the upper door: 900 talents.

Location 4
On the mound of Koḥlit: vessels of contribution with a lagin and ephods. All of the contribution and the seventh (-year) hoard and the second tithe is disqualified. Its entrance is at the end of the aqueduct on the north, 6 cubits towards the frigidarium. ΧΑΓ

Location 5
In the shaft of the escape stairs, in the descent to the left, 3 cubits above the bottom: 40 talents of silver.

Location 6
In the salt pit, which is beneath the steps: 42 talents. HN

Location 7

In the cave of the old place of punishment on the third ledge: 65 gold ingots. Θε

Location 8

In a tomb-chamber, which is in the cemetery of the trees, and within it a pit. In it are (sacred) vessels and 70 talents of silver.

Location 9

In the pit that is next to the eastern gate at a distance of 15 cubits: in it are (sacred) vessels.

Location 10

And in the conduit, in which are ten talents. ΔI

Location 11

In the pit that is under the wall, on the eastern side, in a tooth of the rock: six jars of silver. Its entrance is under the big threshold.

Location 12

In the pool that is east of Koḥlit, in the northern corner, dig 4 cubits: 22 talents.

Location 13

In the cour[t of ...]t, 9 cubits beneath the southern corner: silver and gold vessels of contribution— sprinkling bowls, chalices, libation bowls, ewers—609 in all.

Location 14

Under the other, eastern corner, dig 16 cubits: 40 talents of silver. TP

Location 15

In a cavity, which is in the junction on its north side: vessels

of contribution and clothing. Its entrance is under the western corner.

Location 16

In a tomb, which is in the junction of its east side, on the north, 3 cubits beneath the deceased: 13 talents.

Location 17

In a large pit [... Ko]ḥlit with a column on its north side [...] 14 talents. ΣK

Location 18

In the aqueduct that ent[ers ...] ... as you go, four[tee]n cubits: 55 silver talents.

Location 19

Between the two chambers that are in the Valley of Achor, midway between them, dig 3 cubits: two pots are there, filled with silver.

Location 20

In the cavity of soil, which is at the mouth of the (Wadi) ʿAṣla: 200 silver talents.

Location 21

In the eastern cavity, which is north of Koḥlit: 70 silver talents.

Location 22

In the pile of stones, which is in the Valley of Secacah, dig 1 cubit: 12 silver talents.

Location 23

At the top of the aqueduct, [which ...] Secacah, on the north, und[er the] large [...], dig [thre]e cubits: 7 silver talents.

Location 24

In the fissure, which is in Secacah, east of Solomon's reservoir: vessels of contribution and with an accounting alongside them.

Location 25

Above Solomon's canal, 60 cubits in the direction of the large boulder, dig 3 cubits: 23 silver talents.

Location 26

In a grave, which is in the Wadi Kippa', on the way from Jericho to Secacah, dig 7 cubits: 32 talents.

Location 27

In the cave of the column, which has two entrances, oriented to the east, at the northern entrance, dig 3 cubits: there is a basin with a single book in it. Under it are 42 talents.

Location 28

In the cave, which is at the base of the boulder, which is oriented to the east, dig 9 cubits in the entrance: 21 talents.

Location 29

In the residence of the queen, on the west side, dig 12 cubits: 27 talents.

Location 30

In the cairn that is in the ford of the high priest, d[ig ...] 9 [... cubi]ts: 22 [...] talents.

Location 31

In the aqueduct [...] of the north[ern] reservoir [...] on four sides of ... measure 24 cubits: 400 talents.

Location 32

In the cave that is next to the cooling place belonging to the house of Hakkoz, dig 6 cubits: six jars of silver.

Location 33

At Dok, under the eastern corner of the spreading floor, dig 7 cubits: 22 talents.

Location 34

At the mouth of the water outlet of Kozeba, dig 3 cubits in the direction of the overflow: 80 talents, two gold talents.

Location 35

[In] the aqueduct that is on the road east of the storehouse, which is east of [...]: vessels of contribution and documents. [...]

Location 36

In the outer valley, amid the outflow over the stone, dig 17 cubits: beneath it are 17 talents of silver and gold.

Location 37

In the pile of stones, which is at the entrance of the gorge of the Kidron, dig 3 cubits: four talents.

Location 38

In the stubblefield of the Shaveh facing west, in the southern part, in the grave facing north, dig 24 cubits: 66 talents.

Location 39

In the irrigated field of the Shaveh, in the cairn that is in it, dig 11 cubits, 70 silver talents.

Location 40

In a sluice that is at the base of the Naṭoph, measured from its base 63 cubits, dig 7 cubits: four jars (containing) staters.

Location 41

In the parcel of the [...], in the tomb facing east, dig 8.5 cubits: 23.5 talents.

Location 42

Among the tombs of the Horites, in the open space that faces south, in the gutter, dig 16 [cubits]: 22 talents.

Location 43

In the funnel: a great quantity of sacrificial silver.

Location 44

In the enclosure of the waters that are close to the vault of the drain, at the broad place at their outflow, dig 7 cubits: nine talents.

Location 45

In a cavity, which is north of the entrance of the gorge of Beth-tamar, in the parched surface of some cracked plaster: everything that is in it is consecrated.

Location 46

In the sluice that is at the boundary in the distr[ict of the] south, on the second story, going down from above: nine talents.

Location 47

In the plastered pit of conduits, which are filled from the large wadi, at its bottom: 12 talents.

Location 48

In the reservoir of Beth ha-Kerem, as you go to the left 10 [cubits]: silver, 62 talents.

Location 49

In the basin that is in the valley of [...], in the tomb of its source, a black stone 2 cubits (away); it is the entry: 300 talents of gold and 20 indemnity vessels.

Location 50

Under Absalom's Monument, on the west side, dig 12 [cubits]: 80 talents.

Location 51

In the outflow of the waters of [...], under the trough: 17 talents.

Location 52

In the courtyard (of the tomb) of Zadok, at their four corner buttresses: vessels of contribution with an accounting alongside them.

Location 53

Under the southern corner of the portico, in the tomb of Zadok, under the column of the exedra: vessels of discarded contribution, (that is,) spoiled contribution, and an accounting is alongside them.

Location 54

In the cleared area atop the cliff that looks west, in front of the courtyard of (the tomb of) Zadok, under the large cover which is at its base: it is consecrated material.

Location 55

In the grave that is under the bushes: 40 talents.

Location 56

In the grave of the common people—it is clean. In it are vessels of contribution or spoiled contribution, with an accounting alongside them.

Location 57

In the place of the two reservoirs, in the reservoir as you enter into its little basin: vessels of liquid contribution, (that is,) disqualified contribution, with an accounting alongside them.

Location 58

At the western entrance [...] of the mausoleum, (where there is) an overflow duct alongside the [...] 900: gold talents 5, (silver) talents 60. Its entrance is from the west.

Location 59

Under the black stone: oil flasks.

Location 60

Under the threshold of the crypt: 42 talents.

Location 61

On Mount Gerizim, under the ascent of the upper cavity, one chest and all its vessels, and 60 talents of silver.

Location 62

In the mouth of the well of Beth-[...], silver vessels and gold vessels of contribution and silver. The total is 600 talents.

Location 63

In the large gutter of the crypt: the vessels of the crypt chamber, the total weight: 71 talents, 20 minas.

Location 64

In a cavity that is in the bright place north of Koḥlit, opening to the north, and (where there are) graves at its entrance: a duplicate of this document and an explication and their measurements and a detailed inventory of everything, one by one.

Notes

1 — THE SCHOLARS WIN ONE

[1] Hershel Shanks, ed., *Frank Moore Cross: Conversations with a Bible Scholar* (Washington, DC: Biblical Archaeology Society, 1994), p. 114.

[2] Bargil Pixner, "Unravelling the Copper Scroll Code: A Study on the Topography of 3Q15," *Revue de Qumran*, vol. 11 (1983), p. 334.

2 — FROM ROLLS TO SCROLLS

[1] Joseph A. Fitzmyer, S.J., *The Dead Sea Scrolls: Major Publications and Tools for Study*, rev. ed. (Atlanta: Scholars Press, 1990), p. 191.

[2] K.G. Kuhn, "Les Rouleaux de Cuivre de Qumran," *Revue Biblique*, vol. 61 (1954), p. 197. Translated from the French by Stephanie Audette.

[3] John Marco Allegro, *The Treasure of the Copper Scroll: The Opening and Decipherment of the Most Mysterious of the Dead Sea Scrolls, a Unique Inventory of Buried Treasure*, 1st ed. (Garden City, NY: Doubleday, 1960), p. 20. This edition differs from the second edition published in 1964.

[4] John Marco Allegro, *The Treasure of the Copper Scroll: The Opening and Decipherment of the Most Mysterious of the Dead Sea Scrolls, a Unique Inventory of Buried Treasure, with Some of the Results of a Survey Carried Out on the Treasure Sites in the Holy Land*, 2nd ed. (Garden City, NY: Anchor/Doubleday, 1964), p. 4.

[5] Quoted in William Johnson, "Professor Henry Wright Baker: The Copper Scroll and His Career," in George J. Brooke and Philip R. Davies, eds., *Copper Scroll Studies,* Journal for the Study of the Pseudepigrapha Supplement Series 40 (London and New York: Sheffield Academic Press, 2002), p. 38.

[6] Johnson, "Professor Henry Wright Baker" (see endnote 5), p. 38.

[7] See Yigael Yadin, *The Message of the Scrolls* (New York: Simon and Schuster, 1957), p. 157.

[8] Allegro, *The Treasure of the Copper Scroll* (1964) (see endnote 4), p. 7.

[9] Allegro, *The Treasure of the Copper Scroll* (1964) (see endnote 4), p. 8.

[10] H. Wright Baker, "Notes on the Opening of the 'Bronze' Scrolls from Qumran," *Bulletin of the John Rylands Library*, vol. 39 (1956), pp. 45–55.

[11] Baker, "Notes on the Opening of the 'Bronze' Scrolls from Qumran," (see endnote 10), p. 54.

[12] Al Wolters, *The Copper Scroll: Overview, Text and Translation* (Sheffield, England: Sheffield Academic Press, 1996), p. 10.

[13] Bargil Pixner, "Unravelling the Copper Scroll Code: A Study on the Topography of 3Q15," *Revue de Qumran*, vol. 11 (1983), p. 326.

3 — SQUABBLING SCHOLARS

[1] John Marco Allegro, *The Treasure of the Copper Scroll*, 2nd ed. (Garden City, NY: Doubleday, 1964), p. 33.

[2] Hershel Shanks, ed., *Frank Moore Cross: Conversations with a Bible Scholar* (Washington, DC: Biblical Archaeology Society, 1994), pp. 142, 144.

[3] Shanks, *Frank Moore Cross* (see endnote 2), pp. 145–146.

[4] J.M. Allegro, Broadcast Talk for BBC Northern Home Service, January 16, 23 and 31, 1956, as noted in Judith Anne Brown, *John Marco Allegro: The Maverick of the Dead Sea Scrolls* (Grand Rapids, MI: William B. Eerdmans, 2005), p. 77.

[5] Allegro, *The Treasure of the Copper Scroll* (1964) (see endnote 1), p. 15.

[6] See Philip R. Davies, "John Allegro and the Copper Scroll," in George J. Brooke and Philip R. Davies, eds., *Copper Scroll Studies,* Journal for the Study of the Pseudepigrapha Supplement Series 40 (London and New York: Sheffield Academic Press, 2002).

[7] Andre Dupont-Sommer, *The Dead Sea Scrolls: A Preliminary Survey* (Oxford: Basil Blackwell, 1952), p. 99.

[8] Edmund Wilson, *The Scrolls from the Dead Sea* (New York: Oxford University Press, 1955).

[9] Wilson, *The Scrolls from the Dead Sea* (see endnote 8), p. 95.

[10] Wilson, *The Scrolls from the Dead Sea* (see endnote 8), pp. 97–98.

4 — PUBLICATION RIGHTS — AND WRONGS

[1] The release may be found in the H. Wright Baker, "Notes on the Opening of the 'Bronze' Scrolls from Qumran," *Bulletin of the John Rylands Library*, vol. 39, no. 1 (1956), p. 56.

[2] Quoted in Philip R. Davies, "John Allegro and the Copper Scroll," in George J. Brooke and Philip R. Davies, eds., *Copper Scroll Studies,* Journal

for the Study of the Pseudepigrapha Supplement Series 40 (London and New York: Sheffield Academic Press, 2002), p. 34.

[3] Quoted in Davies, "John Allegro and the Copper Scroll" (see endnote 2), p. 29.

[4] Judith Anne Brown, *John Marco Allegro: The Maverick of the Dead Sea Scrolls* (Grand Rapids, MI: William B. Eerdmans, 2005), p. 90.

[5] His lecture is reprinted in H. Wright Baker, "Notes on the Opening of the 'Bronze' Scrolls from Qumran" (see endnote 1), pp. 45–56.

[6] John Marco Allegro, *The Treasure of the Copper Scroll*, 2nd ed. (Garden City, NY: Anchor/Doubleday, 1964), p. 31.

[7] Brown, *John Marco Allegro: The Maverick of the Dead Sea Scrolls* (see endnote 4), p. 102.

[8] (Harmondsworth, Middlesex, England: Penguin Books).

[9] Davies, "John Allegro and the Copper Scroll" (see endnote 2), p. 34.

[10] Revised under the title *The Dead Sea Scrolls: A Reappraisal*, 2nd ed. See also Davies, "John Allegro and the Copper Scroll" (see endnote 2), p. 34.

[11] Brown, *John Marco Allegro* (see endnote 4), pp. 100–101.

[12] J.T. Milik, "The Copper Document from Cave III, Qumran," *Biblical Archaeologist*, vol. 19 (1956), p. 60.

[13] J.T. Milik, "The Travail d'Édition des Manuscrits du Désert de Juda." *Supplements to Vetus Testamentum*, vol. 4 (1957), p. 22.

[14] J.T. Milik, "Le Rouleau de Cuivre de Qumrân (3Q 15). Traduction et Commentaire Topographique," *Revue Biblique*, vol. 66, no. 3 (1959), p. 321.

[15] J.T. Milik, "The Copper Document from Cave III of Qumran: Translation and Commentary," *Annual of the Department of Antiquities of Jordan*, vols. 4–5 (1960), p. 137.

[16] George Brooke thinks this was the case. (Personal communication.)

[17] John M. Allegro, *The Treasure of the Copper Scroll*, 1st ed. (Garden City, NY: Doubleday, 1960).

[18] M. Baillet, J.T. Milik and R. de Vaux, *Les 'Petites Grottes' de Qumran, Discoveries in the Judaean Desert of Jordan*, vol. 3 (Oxford: Clarendon Press, 1962).

[19] Brown, *John Marco Allegro* (see endnote 4), p. 277.

[20] Davies, "John Allegro and the Copper Scroll" (see endnote 2), p. 32.

[21] Allegro, *The Treasure of the Copper Scroll* (1964) (see endnote 6), p. 35. In *The Treasure of the Copper Scroll* (1960), p. 6, Allegro claims that three

successive new directors of the department, Dr. Ghuraibi, Said Durra and Dr. Awni Dajani, invited him to publish the text of the Copper Scroll.

Roland de Vaux contests the authority of the directors of Jordan's Antiquities Department to assign to Allegro the right to publish the Copper Scroll. See R. de Vaux, Book Review, *Revue Biblique*, vol. 68 (1961), p. 146.

5 — FOLKLORE OR TEMPLE TREASURE?

[1] Stephan Gorenson, "Sectarianism, Geography, and the Copper Scroll," *Journal of Semitic Studies*, vol. 43 (1992), p. 284.

[2] See Frank Moore Cross, Jr., *The Ancient Library of Qumran & Modern Biblical Studies*, rev. ed. (1980 reprint) (Grand Rapids, MI: Baker Book House, 1961), p. 22. In a 2006 interview with me, he reaffirmed his position that the treasure of the Copper Scroll is traditional and legendary, not historical.

[3] November 12, 2006, at his home in Lexington, Massachusetts. I have since learned that Israeli Scroll scholars Hanan Eshel and Ze'ev Safrai also believe the treasure is fictional.

[4] Al Wolters, *The Copper Scroll: Overview, Text and Translation* (Sheffield, England: Sheffield Acaemic Press, 1996), p. 12.

[5] P. Kyle McCarter, Jr., "The Mystery of the Copper Scroll," in Hershel Shanks, ed., *Understanding the Dead Sea Scrolls* (New York: Random House, 1992), p. 237.

[6] Judah K. Lefkovits, *The Copper Scroll—3Q15: A Reevaluation* (Leiden: Brill, 2000), p. 462.

[7] Michael O. Wise, "David J. Wilmot and the Copper Scroll," in George Brooke and Philip Davies, eds. *Copper Scroll Studies,* Journal for the Study of the Pseudepigrapha Supplement Series 40 (London and New York: Sheffield Academic Press, 2002), p. 304.

[8] Wise, "David J. Wilmot and the Copper Scroll" (see endnote 7), p. 304.

[9] Bargil Pixner, "Unravelling the Copper Scroll Code: A Study on the Topography of 3Q15," *Revue de Qumran*, vol. 11 (1983), p. 326.

[10] David Wilmot quoted in Wise, "David J. Wilmot and the Copper Scroll" (see endnote 7), p. 292.

[11] J.T. Milik, "The Copper Document from Cave III, Qumran," *Biblical Archaeologist*, Vol. 19 (1956), pp. 60-64. Although Milik regarded the list as folklore, he regarded the items as treasures of the Temple. See Milik, *Les 'Petites Grottes' de Qumran, Discoveries in the Judaean Desert of Jordan*, vol. 3 (Oxford: Clarendon Press, 1962), p. 280.

[12] Milik, "The Copper Document from Cave III, Qumran" (see endnote 11).

[13] Lefkovits, *The Copper Scroll—3Q15: A Reevaluation* (see endnote 6), p. 488.

[14] Michael O. Wise, in Michael Wise, Martin Abegg, Jr. and Edward Cook, *Dead Sea Scrolls: A New Translation* (HarperSanFrancisco, 1996).

[15] Florentino Garcia Martinez, *The Dead Sea Scrolls Translated*, 2nd ed. (Leiden: Brill and Grand Rapids, MI: William B. Eerdmans, 1996).

[16] Alan R. Millard, "Does the Bible Exaggerate King Solomon's Golden Wealth?" *Biblical Archaeology Review*, May/June 1989.

[17] McCarter, "The Mystery of the Copper Scroll" (see endnote 5), p. 235.

[18] McCarter, "The Mystery of the Copper Scroll" (see endnote 5), p. 235.

[19] 2 Maccabees 5:21.

[20] Josephus, *Antiquities of the Jews* (Loeb edition) 14.105.

[21] Josephus, *War*, 6.317.

[22] J.T. Milik, "The Copper Document from Cave III, Qumran" (see endnote 11).

[23] Geza Vermes, *The Complete Dead Sea Scrolls in English* (NY: Allen Lane Penguin Press, 1997) p. 585.

[24] Martinez, *The Dead Sea Scrolls Translated* (see endnote 15), p. 461.

[25] Wise, Abegg and Cook, *The Dead Sea Scrolls: A New Translation* (see endnote 14), p. 191.

[26] I am indebted to Kyle McCarter for the information on the House of Hakkoz. See his "The Mystery of the Copper Scroll" (see endnote 5), pp. 238–239.

[27] Emile Puech of the Ecole Biblique in Jerusalem, who has published a new translation of the Copper Scroll (see Chapter 8, endnote 1) is of the view that the treasure is that of the Essenes. See his "Some Results of a New Examination of the Copper Scroll (3Q15)," in Brooke and Davies, eds., *Copper Scroll Studies* (see endnote 7), p. 58.

[28] Al Wolters, *The Copper Scroll* (see endnote 4), p. 12.

[29] Lefkovits, *The Copper Scroll—3Q15: A Reevaluation* (see endnote 6), pp. 498–504.

[30] Wolters, *The Copper Scroll* (see endnote 4), p. 12.

[31] Puech, "Some Results of a New Examination of the Copper Scroll (3Q15)" (see endnote 27), p. 61.

6 — LOCATING THE TREASURE

[1] John Marco Allegro, *The Treasure of the Copper Scroll*, 2nd ed. (Garden City, NY: Anchor Books/Doubleday, 1964), Plate 30.

[2] Allegro, *The Treasure of the Copper Scroll* (1964), Plates 30 and 31.

[3] John Marco Allegro, *The Treasure of the Copper Scroll*, 1st ed. (Garden City, NY: Doubleday, 1960), p. 107.

[4] Judith Anne Brown, *John Marco Allegro: The Maverick of the Dead Sea Scrolls* (Grand Rapids, MI: William B. Eerdmans, 2005), pp. 129–131.

[5] Roland de Vaux, Review, *Revue Biblique*, vol. 68 (1961), pp. 146–147.

[6] Brown, *John Marco Allegro* (see endnote 4), p. 129.

[7] Allegro engaged in two expeditions, one in December 1959/January 1960 and the other in March/April 1960.

[8] P. Kyle McCarter, Jr., s.v. "Geography in the Documents," in Lawrence H. Schiffman and James C. VanderKam, eds., *Encyclopedia of the Dead Sea Scrolls*, vol. 1 (New York: Oxford University Press, 2000), p. 306.

[9] Joel S. Kaminsky, s.v. "Achan," in David Noel Freedman, ed., *Eerdmans Dictionary of the Bible* (Grand Rapids, MI: William B. Eerdmans, 2000), p. 13.

[10] David Merling, s.v. "Achor," in David Noel Freedman, ed., *Eerdmans Dictionary of the Bible* (Grand Rapids, MI: Eerdmans, 2000), p. 13.

[11] Kyle McCarter quoting B. Luria in McCarter's working notes on Copper Scroll translation (1993).

[12] Yitzhak Magen and Yuval Peleg, *The Qumran Excavations, 1993–2004, Preliminary Report* (Jerusalem: Judea and Samaria Publications, 2007), p. 64. Yitzhak Magen's report is summarized in Hershel Shanks, "Qumran—The Pottery Factory," *Biblical Archaeology Review*, September/October 2006.

[13] Oren Gutfeld, "Hyrcania's Mysterious Tunnels," *Biblical Archaeology Review*, September/October 2006.

[14] Shanks, "Qumran—The Pottery Factory" (see endnote 12).

[15] Shanks, "Qumran—The Pottery Factory" (see endnote 12).

[16] Allegro, *The Treasure of the Copper Scroll* (1964) (see endnote 1), pp. 57–58.

[17] Michael Wise, Martin Abegg, Jr. and Edward Cook, *The Dead Sea Scrolls: A New Translation* (HarperSanFrancisco, 1996), p. 190.

[18] Brown, *John Marco Allegro* (see endnote 4), p. 125.

[19] Bargil Pixner, "Unravelling the Copper Scroll Code: A Study on the Topography of 3Q15," *Revue de Qumran*, vol. 11 (1983), p. 327.

[20] Josephus, *War* 6:390–391.

[21] This story is recounted in Wise, Abegg and Cook, *The Dead Sea Scrolls* (see endnote 17), p. 190.

7 — T U N N E L   M Y S T E R Y

[1] G.R.H. Wright, "The Archaeological Remains at El Mird in the Wilderness of Judaea," *Biblica*, vol. 42, Fasc. 1 (1961), pp. 1–21.

[2] John Marco Allegro, *The Treasure of the Copper Scroll*, 2nd ed. (Garden City, NY: Anchor/Doubleday, 1964), p. 61.

[3] Allegro, *The Treasure of the Copper Scroll* (1964) (see endnote 2), p. 60.

[4] All quotes from Bob Morgan are from his unpublished "The Mount Hyrcania Project: Preliminary Report" (n.d.), a copy of which the author graciously provided. It is dedicated to John Allegro's widow, Joan R. Allegro. In addition, I interviewed Morgan several times by telephone.

[5] The Hebrew is *petach*, literally "opening." Some translations render "gate" or "gateway." Others translate the word as "door." The Jewish Publication Society translation has "plowland" and relates the Hebrew, not to "open," but to *pittach*, "to plow."

[6] Oren Gutfeld, "Hyrcania's Mysterious Tunnels: Searching for the Treasures of the Copper Scroll," *Biblical Archaeology Review*, September/October 2006.

[7] Oren Gutfeld, s.v. "Hyrcania," in Ephraim Stern, ed., *The New Encyclopedia of Archaeological Excavations in the Holy Land*, vol. 5 (Jerusalem and Washington: Israel Exploration Society and Biblical Archaeology Society, forthcoming).

8 — S A V I N G   T H E   S C R O L L

[1] This chapter is based largely on Régis Bertholon, Noël Lacoudre and Jorge Vasquez, "The Conservation and Restoration of the Copper Scroll from Qumran," in George J. Brooke and Philip R. Davies, eds., *Copper Scroll Studies,* Journal for the Study of the Pseudepigrapha, Supplement Series 40 (Sheffield, England: Sheffield Academic Press, 2002), reprinted in Daniel Brizemeure, Noel Lacoudre and Emile Puech *Le Rouleau de cuivre de la grotte 3 de Qumrân (3Q15): Expertise—Restauration—Epigraphie* vol. I & vol. II (École Biblique et Archéologique Française de Jérusalem, Brill and EDF Foundation, 2006).

[2] Brizemeure, Lacoudre and Puech, *Le Rouleau de cuivre de la grotte 3 de Qumrân (3Q15)* (see endnote 1).

Bibliography

John Marco Allegro, *The People of the Dead Sea Scrolls in Text and Pictures* (Garden City, NY: Doubleday, 1958).

John Marco Allegro, *The Treasure of the Copper Scroll: The Opening and Decipherment of the Most Mysterious of the Dead Sea Scrolls, a Unique Inventory of Buried Treasure* (Garden City, NY: Doubleday, 1960).

John Marco Allegro, *The Treasure of the Copper Scroll: The Opening and Decipherment of the Most Mysterious of the Dead Sea Scrolls, a Unique Inventory of Buried Treasure, with Some of the Results of a Survey Carried Out on the Treasure Sites in the Holy Land*, 2nd ed. (Garden City NY: Anchor/Doubleday, 1964).

John Marco Allegro, *Search in the Desert* (Garden City, NY: Doubleday, 1964).

M. Baillet, J.T. Milik and R. de Vaux, *Les "Petites Grottes" de Qumran, Discoveries in the Judaean Desert of Jordan*, vol. 3. (Oxford: Clarendon Press, 1962).

H. Wright Baker, "Notes on the Opening of the 'Bronze' Scrolls from Qumran," *Bulletin of the John Rylands Library*, vol. 39, no. 1 (1956), pp. 45–56.

Daniel Brizemeure, Noel Lacoudre and Emile Puech, *Le Rouleau de cuivre de la grotte 3 de Qumrân (3Q15): Expertise—Restauration—Epigraphie*, Vol. I & Vol. II (École Biblique et Archéologique Française de Jérusalem, Brill and EDF Foundation, 2006).

George Brooke and Philip Davies, eds., *Copper Scroll Studies* Journal for the Study of the Pseudepigrapha Supplement Series 40 (London and New York: Sheffield Academic Press, 2002).

Judith Anne Brown, *John Marco Allegro: The Maverick of the Dead Sea Scrolls* (Grand Rapids, MI: William B. Eerdmans, 2005).

Frank Moore Cross, Jr., *The Ancient Library of Qumran & Modern Biblical Studies*, rev. ed. (1980 reprint) (Grand Rapids, MI: Baker Book House, 1961).

Andre Dupont-Sommer, *The Dead Sea Scrolls: A Preliminary Survey* (Oxford: Basil Blackwell, 1952).

Oren Gutfeld, "Hyrcania's Mysterious Tunnels: Searching for the Treasures of the Copper Scroll," *Biblical Archaeology Review*, September/October 2006.

Karl George Kuhn, "Les rouleaux de cuivre de Qumran," *Revue Biblique*, vol. 61 (1954), pp. 193–205.

Judah K. Lefkovits, *The Copper Scroll (3Q15): A Reevaluation* (Leiden & Boston: Brill, 2000).

Florentino Garcia Martinez, *The Dead Sea Scrolls Translated*, 2nd ed. (Leiden: Brill; Grand Rapids, MI: William B. Eerdmans, 1996).

Józef T. Milik, "The Copper Document from Cave III, Qumran" *Biblical Archaeologist*, vol. 19 (1956), pp. 60–64.

Józef Milik, "Le travail d'edition des manuscrits du Désert de Juda," *Supplement to Vetus Testamentum*, vol. 4 (1957), pp. 17–26.

Józef T. Milik, "Le rouleau de cuivre de Qumran (3Q15)," *Revue Biblique*, vol. 66, no. 3 (1959), pp. 550–575.

J.T. Milik, *Ten Years of Discovery in the Wilderness of Judaea*, translated by J. Strugnell (London: SCM, 1959).

J.T. Milik, "The Copper Document from Cave III of Qumran: Translation and Commentary," *Annual of the Department of Antiquities of Jordan*, vols. 4–5 (1960), pp. 137–155.

Robert Morgan, "The Mount Hyrcania Project: Preliminary Report" (n.d.), unpublished.

Bargil Pixner, "Unravelling the Copper Scroll Code: A Study on the Topography of 3Q15," *Revue de Qumran*, vol. 11 (1983), pp. 323–361, + plans i–iv.

Hershel Shanks, ed., *Understanding the Dead Sea Scrolls* (New York: Random House, 1992).

Hershel Shanks, ed., *Frank Moore Cross: Conversations with a Bible Scholar* (Washington, DC: Biblical Archaeology Society, 1994).

Hershel Shanks, "Qumran—The Pottery Factory," *Biblical Archaeology Review*, September/October 2006.

Edmund Wilson, *The Scrolls from the Dead Sea* (New York: Oxford University Press, 1955).

Michael Wise, Martin Abegg, Jr. and Edward Cook, *Dead Sea Scrolls—A New Translation* (HarperSanFrancisco, 1996).

G.R.H. Wright, "The Archaeological Remains at El Mird in the Wilderness of Judaea," *Biblica*, vol. 42, Fasc. 1 (1961), pp. 1–21.

Al Wolters, *The Copper Scroll: Overview, Text and Translation* (Sheffield, England: Sheffield Academic Press, 1996).

Illustration Credits